THE
HEBRIDEAN
BAKER
at Home

HEBRIDEAN
BAKER

THE HEBRIDEAN BAKER

at Home

COINNEACH MACLEOD

PHOTOGRAPHY BY SUSIE LOWE

sourcebooks

Published by Sourcebooks
P.O. Box 4410, Naperville, Illinois 60567-4410
(630) 961-3900
sourcebooks.com

Originally published in 2023 in the United Kingdom by Black & White Publishing Ltd, a division of Bonnier Books UK.

Printed and bound in China.

BWP 10 9 8 7 6 5 4 3 2 1

A Phàdruig

Together we've created amazing stories.
Here's to the chapters yet unwritten and
the journey that lies ahead.

Tha gaol agam ort, Coinneach x

CONTENTS

1 • SCOTTISH BAKES

2 • FROM CROFT TO TABLE

3 • JUST A WEE TREAT

4 • CELTIC BAKES

5 • A SPOONFUL OF HYGGE

6 • DRAMS & DEOCHS

7 • HOME COMFORTS

8 • AN ISLAND CHRISTMAS

FÀILTE

Fàilte friends, welcome to my Hebridean home! In my kitchen, flavours become stories, bakes become family favourites and recipes are shared with friends from across the islands. My kitchen is my haven, my slice of paradise, where I sing along with my stirring, dance with my sourdough and take delight in testing lots of new recipes. I'm excited to share this with you.

Join me where the rolling hills of the Hebrides meet the rolling pins of my kitchen!

This book is an invitation to experience the love I have for my kitchen and my island, through the lens of my own heartfelt journey. So, whether you're a seasoned baker, an intrepid food lover, or simply someone seeking a taste of the Hebrides, I invite you to embark on this delightful culinary adventure with me.

For this book, I travelled from Islay, via Barra, Uist, Berneray and Harris before arriving home to Lewis, meeting friends and family along the way and learning what home means to them and what they love to bake in their kitchens. They have generously shared recipes and stories that have been handed down through the generations, bakes that celebrate the flavours of Scotland and simple dishes that you can whip up from your store cupboard ingredients. These recipes are meant to be shared and savoured; I hope they will become woven into the fabric of your own cherished moments.

This cookbook is more than simply a collection of recipes, it beckons you to uncover the stories that breathe life into each dish. Beyond the culinary delights, these pages are an ode to the joy of gathering around a table, exchanging tales, and creating lasting memories. This is a journey to celebrate the Hebrides itself – the rugged landscapes, the vibrant Gaelic culture, the spirit of its people. I will share with you the essence of the Hebrides, and how it has shaped my identity as a baker and a lover of all things culinary.

I hope I will also inspire you to take off on your own adventure to the islands. I have asked my friends to tell me their favourite nooks around the Hebrides. From Colonsay to Taransay, some of these spots might not be found in the travel guides, but if you venture off the beaten path, you might find a rocky shoreline, a heather-topped hill or a wee island only accessible at low tide to fall in love with.

And fear not, I have not forgotten the simple pleasures in life. Within these pages, you will find perfect biscuits to dunk in your tea, comforting desserts that evoke memories of bygone days, cakes that will be sliced when visitors come to stay and hearty dishes that will warm up a winter's evening. Oh, and of course, plenty of memorable moments with Seòras the West Highland terrier and Peter, the official Hebridean Baker's cake taster!

So, dear reader, fasten your apron, switch on your oven, and prepare to embark on an adventure that will transport you from your very own kitchen to the heart of the Hebrides. Welcome to my home. Welcome to my kitchen.

HINTS & TIPS

Throughout *The Hebridean Baker*, I use certain preparation and baking techniques that I have learned work for me, but you might have your own way that works just as well. I'd love you to put a twist on my recipes!

When I list the following basics for a recipe, unless stated otherwise, I'd like you to use:

- **Butter.** Unsalted and softened.
- **Eggs.** Medium.
- **Milk.** Whole.
- **Oats.** Rolled.
- **Sugar.** Caster.

Most of my ingredients should be readily available. If they aren't, normally there is an easy replacement, or they have another name. For example, you can substitute or replace as follows:

- **Black treacle** with blackstrap molasses.
- **Double cream** with whipping cream.
- **Mixed spice** with pumpkin spice mix.
- **Vanilla bean paste** with vanilla extract.
- **Bicarbonate of soda** is baking soda.
- **Caster sugar** is superfine or baker's sugar.
- **Icing sugar** is powdered sugar.
- **Ground almonds** are almond flour.
- **Cornflour** is corn starch.
- **Plain flour** is all-purpose flour.
- **Golden syrup** has no equivalent! Search high and low!

A note about caster sugar: some recipes call for golden caster sugar. If you can't find it, the main difference between the two sugars is the colour and a slightly more caramel taste to the golden caster sugar. It will not affect the bake too much, so you can stick to caster sugar if need be.

Lots of classic cake recipes begin with creaming butter and sugar together until pale and fluffy. Use an electric whisk on its slowest speed initially, then increase the speed to create a light and fluffy mixture. You can use a wooden spoon, but this will take much longer – and a lot more effort!

And, when melting your chocolate, if you don't have a microwave, place a small saucepan a quarter filled with water onto a very gentle simmer. Place a heatproof bowl on top without it touching the water. Break up the chocolate and add to the bowl, then stir regularly until melted.

And finally, although I have tried to convert the measurements – I do recommend that you purchase digital kitchen scales. They are life changing!

STORNOWAY BLACK PUDDING

BY:

Charles Macleod

Ropework Park
Stornoway, HS 1 2LB
01851 702445

Ingredients: Beef Suet,
Vegetable Fat, **Oatmeal (Gluten)**,
Pork Blood, Onions, Salt, Spices.
Allergen Information: **in bold**

GEOGRAPHIC ORIGIN
UK PROTECTED

UK WA 037

1.3 kg ℮

great taste 2019

COINNEACH'S LARDER

I am passionate about using home-grown Hebridean and Scottish produce. Eating locally first means choosing food that is grown and harvested close to where you live, investing in the local community and its people. Here are some of my favourite producers of quality foods that I use in my home. I'd love you to give them a try!

JURA WHISKY
JURAWHISKY.COM

The wee island of Jura distils my favourite dram; their range complements the bakes, cocktails and recipes in this book perfectly. Treat yourself to a bottle of their eighteen-year-old whisky; it's my favourite!

ISLE OF HARRIS DISTILLERY
HARRISDISTILLERY.COM

The distillery opened in 2015 in the village of Tarbert, on the Isle of Harris. You can take guided tours and visit the shop to buy a bottle or two of Harris Gin. Flavoured with local, hand-harvested sugar kelp, it comes in a beautifully distinctive bottle.

LOCH DUART SALMON
LOCHDUART.COM

When selecting salmon for my kitchen, I always choose Loch Duart. Their salmon are grown in the cold, clear waters of northwest Scotland, giving them a beautiful colour and a firmer texture.

STAG BAKERIES
STAGBAKERIES.CO.UK

This artisan bakery in Stornoway uses traditional methods and only the finest ingredients. And it's where you can order the range of Hebridean Baker shortbread and oaty biscuits!

CHARLES MACLEOD BUTCHER
CHARLESMACLEOD.CO.UK

For the finest Stornoway Black Pudding and the warmest welcome on the island, visit the iconic Charlie Barley's shop in Stornoway on the Isle of Lewis. Made to the original seventy-year-old recipe, their black puddings are legendary.

HIGHLAND STONEWARE
HIGHLANDSTONEWARE.COM

Highland Stoneware pottery is situated in the northwest Highlands of Scotland. From making their own clay to the finished pot, each piece is individually hand painted by a team of craftspeople in Lochinver and Ullapool.

ERIBÉ KNITWEAR
ERIBE.COM

Not in my larder, but definitely in my wardrobe – and I wear them every day! ERIBÉ puts a contemporary twist on traditional Scottish knitwear and heritage knitting techniques such as Fair Isle.

MY HEBRIDES

'Coinneach, c'mon, we're off on an adventure!' said Peter, pulling on his Wellington boots and throwing a backpack full of picnic treats over his shoulder.

It's only a few miles from his family home in Oban to the pier at Gallanach and from there we hopped on the CalMac ferry taking its twelve passengers the five-minute journey over to the beautiful Hebridean island of Kerrera. We step off the ferry and begin our hike to the other side of the island.

Peter tells me the story of King Alexander II of Scotland that appears in the thirteenth-century Old Norse saga *Hákonar saga Hákonarsonar*. In a dream, Alexander is warned by the three saints Columba, Olaf and Magnus not to invade the Norwegian-held islands of the Hebrides. He decides to ignore the words of these saintly men and mounts a military campaign to take the isles by force in 1249. However, days later, Alexander falls ill and dies on the island of Kerrera. The saga portrays his death as a divine punishment for making the Norse gods angry!

Gylen Castle, built in 1582 by the MacDougalls, sits on the edge of a rocky ridge at the southern end of Kerrera. It barely managed sixty years of occupation before it was besieged and burned down in 1647. As we sit with our picnic by the castle, Peter looks out onto the Isle of Seil and the Isle of Mull, the two Hebridean islands his mum and dad were brought up on. There's still time to stop in for a cuppa at the Kerrera Tea Garden before we head over the hills to the ferry, safe in the knowledge that the Norse gods have granted us a reprieve from their fury . . . this time!

Everyone has their own favourite wee secret getaway in the Hebrides, be it one that brings back a childhood memory, a place you return to every year for a holiday or for that perfect Instagram photo. Mountains, moors and machair, white sandy beaches, bothies and cèilidhs – they make folk return to the islands time and again. So, I asked my friends to share their favourite destinations in the Hebrides.

Karen Matheson: Scottish musician and lead singer of multi-award-winning folk band Capercaillie.
A couple of summers ago, I fulfilled a dream of visiting the most secluded of all the Small Isles. Hidden from mainland view by the towering mountains of Rum, the Isle of Canna had long held a fascination for me, home to the wonderful collection of folk songs collected by John Lorne Campbell and Margaret Faye Shaw that are now held in Canna House. I later learned that I had ancestors back in the late 1700s from Canna

and so the visit was even more poignant. From the dramatic coastal cliffs, fascinating churches and deserted beaches to the puffin colony on the neighbouring island of Sanday. Oh, and our hosts cooked us fresh lobster straight from the pier . . . haste me back!

Janice Forsyth: commentator and presenter of arts broadcasting in Scotland, host of *The Afternoon Show* on BBC Radio Scotland.
The island of Bute has had a place in my heart since I was a toddler playing on Rothesay beach. My parents even had their honeymoon there! The emotional pull of Bute feels like it's written into my DNA, and I'm old enough to remember the excitement of joining the queue at glorious Wemyss Bay Station, with hundreds of other excited working-class Glaswegian families for our sail *doon the watter*, in the days before package holidays abroad.

It was our annual adventure! But because we didn't have a car on the island, we stayed in Rothesay, never venturing further afield. So, it was many years before I discovered my favourite place on Bute – wonderful Scalpsie Bay. My brother Roddy and I had gone for a day trip during a blistering heatwave and hitched a lift; seeing the bay was love at first sight. A short walk along a sandy path revealed an astonishing sight. Hundreds of seals lay on rocks basking in the sun and across the water was a spectacular view of Arran. I'll never forget that first visit, but I feel a similar thrill every time I go there.

Eilidh Cormack: Royal National Mòd Gold Medallist, Gaelic Singer of the Year and one third of the all-female Gaelic group Sian.
They say west is best and, for me, it really is true. Head as far along the winding Waternish road on the Isle of Skye as you can, and you'll hit Trumpan. The ruined church here was the scene of a brutal clan massacre.

One Sunday in 1578, while MacLeods worshipped inside the church, the MacDonalds of Uist landed in the bay and set fire to its thatched roof. I should make clear that this was in retaliation after the Isle of Eigg gained a new landmark known as Massacre Cave! One young girl managed to escape and raise the alarm, the MacLeods' Fairy Flag was unfurled, and *Blàr Milleadh a' Ghàrraidh* (the Battle of the Spoiled Dyke) ensued.

This is one of my favourite places in the world – not only for its dark history (and dark skies, being one of the best places for spotting the Northern Lights on the island), but for its stunning views out to Ardmore Bay, the cliffs at Dunvegan Head and the Outer Hebrides.

Anna Campbell-Jones: interior designer and judge on BBC's *Scotland's Home of the Year*.
I have been visiting Gigha since I was a teenager, and recently my partner Peter and I were staying at the hotel and we wanted to go for a walk. Seemingly waiting especially for us outside was a sweet-looking dog 'doing a Lassie', so we decided to follow him. After taking us to a tiny beach and instructing us to throw sticks into the sea for him he escorted us to Achamore House; it was clearly a route he knew well – through the stunning gardens verdant with gigantic Gunnera plants and rhododendrons and then through the walled garden, past the peacocks and through a tiny gate in the back wall. He led us up a short steep path through the undergrowth and we three sat down to enjoy the stunning panoramic view. Clearly his favourite spot on Gigha, and now ours. We later found out that Django the dog from Tarbert Farm does this regularly, meeting tourists from the ferry and showing them around his magical wee island!

Joy Dunlop: Scottish singer, stepdancer, host of BBC Alba's *Speak Gaelic* and BBC Scotland weather presenter.

Our summer holidays were always to the Isle of Colonsay, in the Inner Hebrides. The whole family would cram into this tiny cottage for a few weeks, where we'd do nothing except ride our bikes, eat ice cream and visit the beach. Colonsay has many beautiful beaches, but my favourite spot was, and still is, Kiloran Bay; a mile of golden sand and clear blue-green water. It's tranquil and secluded, with the perfect mix of sand dunes, rock pools, warm sand and open sea.

My family aren't known for packing light, and everyone would laden themselves with rucksacks, cool boxes, windbreaks, buckets, spades and more, before making our way to 'our spot'. This was a quiet and peaceful corner, meaning that we could spend the whole day there without bothering anyone. We played in the sun, ate Dairylea cheese and crisp sandwiches and drank cups of tea from multiple Thermoses to warm us post-swimming. Idyllic.

Lesley Riddoch: award-winning broadcaster, author, land reform campaigner, and lover of all things Scottish and Nordic.

Every year (almost) for the last quarter of a century, I've crossed the Minch from Arisaig in the fabulous wee Sheerwater ferry to reach Eigg. The boat is part of the experience. It's skippered by Ronnie Dyer – a local man, who'll point to the basking sharks, dolphins and orcas you'll see en route. Then onto Eigg – or 'edge' in Old Norse, because of the striking basalt ridge that dominates the tiny island. The centre of the island is a moorland plateau, rising to 1,289ft at An Sgùrr. Standing on the summit, you can see the whole west coast of Scotland: mountains, sea lochs, islands and all. And the bonus? You'll have spent three hours on a community-owned island and can now enjoy a pint from their brewery!

Sue Lawrence: Scottish cookery and food writer whose cookbooks include *A Taste of Scotland's Islands* and *A Cook's Tour of Scotland*.

There are so many special places to go on Islay. I love cycling along the Three Distilleries pathway, the sea by my side – and always visit the Celtic House in Bowmore with its brilliant books, great coffee and cakes. But one of the quietest is Loch Gruinart's beaches. On the west side there's Ardnave and Tayvulin; on the east, Killinallan. All of these involve a walk over dunes, lugging your picnic basket and binoculars; the latter essential since you can see otters and seals from the sandy beaches. And, where the sea loch meets the sea, the seals surf playfully along the waves. Beyond them, on a clear day, you can see Colonsay on the horizon.

Now, after all this love for the Inner Hebrides, don't forget to turn to page 101 to be inspired by the islands of the Outer Hebrides!

FERN CAKE

SERVES 8

INGREDIENTS

For the pastry

200g (7oz) plain flour, plus extra for dusting

2 tablespoons icing sugar

100g (3½oz) butter, chilled and diced

1 large egg, beaten

1 tablespoon milk

Pinch of salt

Baking beans for blind baking

For the filling

150g (5oz) butter

150g (5oz) golden caster sugar

3 large eggs, beaten

150g (5oz) ground almonds

½ teaspoon almond extract

1 lemon, zested

4 tablespoons raspberry jam

For the topping

200g (7oz) icing sugar

1 teaspoon almond extract

8 teaspoons water (plus more if necessary)

Food colouring gel, green for the classic fern shape

Fern cake was a beloved staple of local Scottish bakeries in the 1970s and 80s. A nostalgic treat that evokes a sense of charm and simplicity, it's definitely time to bring it back to our kitchen tables. Buttery crisp shortcrust pastry, fruity raspberry jam, squidgy almondy frangipane and a soft iced topping with a delicate fern design. Your Bakewell tart has just had an upgrade!

METHOD

To make the pastry

Sift the flour, icing sugar and a pinch of salt into a large bowl. Then, using your fingertips, rub in the butter until it forms fine crumbs. Add the beaten egg and milk and lightly bring together to form a firm dough, taking care not to handle it any more than necessary. Shape into a disc (which will be easier to roll out later), then chill, wrapped in clingfilm, for 30 minutes.

Roll the pastry out on a lightly floured surface to the thickness of a pound coin. Use it to line a 23cm (9") fluted, loose-bottomed tart tin. Trim the excess and prick all over with a fork. Chill for 30 minutes.

Preheat the oven to 160°C fan (350°F) along with a baking sheet. Place baking paper over the pastry in the tart tin and scatter over the baking beans. Blind bake for 15 minutes, then remove the beans and paper. Cook for a further 5 minutes until pale golden.

To make the filling & topping

Cream the butter and sugar together until pale and fluffy. Beat in the eggs a little at a time, then fold in the ground almonds, almond extract and lemon zest.

Spread the jam evenly across the base of the pastry case, then spoon over the sponge mixture, levelling the surface with the back of the spoon.

Bake for 30 minutes until golden, well risen and just set in the centre. Leave to cool in the tin for 5 minutes, then lift onto a wire rack and cool completely.

To make the topping, put the icing sugar in a mixing bowl with the almond extract. Stir in a teaspoon of water at a time until you have a thick, smooth, spreadable fondant.

Pour the white fondant mixture on top of the tart, taking it to the edge of the crust. Pipe the zigzag fern design with food colouring gel onto the fondant and then drag a toothpick down the lines to create a feathered effect. Allow to set completely before serving.

DOUBLE DRAM CAKE

SERVES 8

INGREDIENTS

For the crémeux

60g (2oz) sugar

80g (2¾oz) egg yolk
(you will need 4 large
egg yolks)

250g (9oz) milk

250g (9oz) double cream

230g (8oz) dark chocolate

40ml (2 tablespoons +
2 teaspoons) whisky

For the cake

50g (1¾oz) dark chocolate

100ml (⅓ cup +
2 tablespoons) milk

30g (1oz) cocoa powder

125g (4½oz) butter

125g (4½oz) sugar

2 large eggs, beaten

1 teaspoon vanilla bean
paste

125g (4½oz) self-raising flour

Pinch of salt

Combining the luscious flavour of dark chocolate and the distinctive warmth of whisky, this whisky chocolate cake is as rich and decadent as you'd hope! This indulgent treat has a moist and tender chocolate cake, layered and topped with a velvety, whisky-infused chocolate crémeux. Yes, the crémeux takes time, but I promise it's worth it. Truly, this is a luxurious hug of a cake!

METHOD

To make the crémeux

Whisk together the sugar and egg yolks in a bowl until light and creamy. Combine the milk and cream in a pan and place over a medium heat, gently heating until just before boiling point. Pour the hot milk and cream over the egg mixture, then return to the pan and cook to 84°C (183°F) until the mixture has slightly thickened to create an anglaise.

Chop the chocolate and place in a bowl, then carefully pour the warm anglaise over the top, mixing thoroughly until the chocolate has melted. Stir in the whisky and allow to cool slightly, then cover with clingfilm and refrigerate (for at least 4 hours) until ready to layer the cake.

To make the cake

Break up the chocolate, add half to a bowl and place in the microwave in bursts of 20 seconds until melted, then add the rest of the chocolate and stir until completely melted and set aside to cool slightly. In a separate bowl, gradually mix the milk with the cocoa powder, combining to make a paste.

Grease and line two 18cm (7") loose-based sponge tins. Preheat the oven to 170°C fan (375°F).

Cream together the butter and sugar until light and fluffy. Add the beaten eggs and vanilla, a little at a time. With a large spoon fold in the flour and a pinch of salt, then fold in the cooled melted chocolate and the cocoa paste.

Divide the cake batter equally between the 2 tins, then bake for 15 to 18 minutes until the cakes are risen and a skewer comes out clean. Cool in the tins for 5 minutes and turn out onto wire racks to cool.

Sandwich the cakes together with half the crémeux, then smooth the rest over the top. Now your double dram cake is ready to serve to your guests.

HEBRIDEAN HYGGE CAKE

SERVES 6

INGREDIENTS

For the cake

225g (8oz) sugar

½ teaspoon vanilla bean paste

3 eggs

225g (8oz) plain flour

2 teaspoons baking powder

75g (2½oz) butter

150ml (½ cup + 2 tablespoons) milk

For the topping

100g (3½oz) butter

150g (5oz) desiccated coconut

250g (9oz) dark brown sugar

75ml (⅓ cup) milk

Pinch of salt

I've brought a wee bit of Denmark back home to the Hebrides! Originating from Hjallerup in Jutland, the recipe dates back to 1960 when a woman named Jytte Andersen took part in a cake-baking competition. Her Drømmekage was so good that it won, and the rest is sweet history.

The star of the show is the irresistible coconut and caramel topping that crowns the Drømmekage. As the cake bakes, the topping caramelises to create a delightful, slightly chewy golden crust. Whether enjoyed with a cup of coffee on a chilly autumnal afternoon or shared with loved ones on special occasions, this cake brings a sense of warmth and togetherness to any gathering.

METHOD

Preheat the oven to 170°C fan (375°F) and grease and line a 20cm (8") cake tin.

Cream together the sugar, vanilla and eggs for at least 4 minutes until light and creamy.

In another bowl, sift the flour and baking powder together. Fold the flour into the egg mixture.

Melt the butter in a pan and add the milk. Pour into the batter you have made, folding it in until it is just combined. Pour the batter into the prepared cake pan.

Bake for about 30 minutes until the cake is nearly cooked.

To make the topping

Meanwhile, simply place all the topping ingredients in a saucepan and stir together until melted. Carefully spread a layer over your nearly cooked cake. Turn up the heat to 200°C fan (425°F) and bake for a further 5 minutes. Cool in the tin for 15 minutes and then turn out onto a wire rack.

Put the kettle on, take a slice and envelop yourself in Hebridean Hygge.

BONNACH STRUGHAIN

SERVES 24

INGREDIENTS

For the scone mix

350g (12½oz) self-raising
flour

110g (4oz) butter, cubed

1 teaspoon baking powder

60g (2oz) sugar

1 egg

200ml (¾ cup +
1 tablespoon) milk

For the treacle batter

4 eggs

120g (4½oz) sugar

250ml (1 cup) milk

4 tablespoons black treacle

450g (1lb) self-raising flour

2 teaspoons baking powder

2 tablespoons vegetable oil

The 29th of September is Michaelmas, signifying the end of the harvest, the start of autumn and the beginning of the shorter days. On the Hebridean islands of Uist and Barra, to celebrate Latha Fhèill Mìcheil it is traditional to bake a Bonnach Strughain the evening before.

I met Theresa over 20 years ago when we sang together in the Glasgow Islay Gaelic Choir. We have been great friends ever since. Theresa is passionate about keeping island traditions alive and here she shares a Bonnach Strughain recipe handed down to her.

METHOD

To make the scone mix

Preheat the oven to 200°C fan (425°F).

Sieve your flour, then add the butter and rub it in lightly with your fingertips until the mixture resembles fine breadcrumbs.

Stir in the baking powder and sugar. Make a well in the mixture, lightly beat an egg before pouring it in along with the milk and then combine quickly with a table knife.

Tip the mixture onto a well-floured surface, gently bring together into a round shape slightly smaller than your ovenproof skillet, dust flour onto the skillet, place the scone on top and bake for 30 minutes until a skewer comes out clean. Leave it in the skillet, though, as you'll be baking it some more.

To make the treacle batter

While the scone is in the oven, prepare the treacle batter. Whisk the eggs in a bowl until light and fluffy, then whisk in the sugar for a further 2 minutes, before adding the milk and the treacle and mix until combined. Add the flour and baking powder a bit at a time, continuing to mix well. Finally mix in the oil.

When the scone comes out of the oven, pour two-thirds of the treacle batter over the top of the cooked scone, spreading it with a palette knife to cover the top and sides. Reduce the oven temperature to 180°C fan (400°F). Place back in to cook for a further 16 minutes.

Now, remove it from the oven. Using a wire rack, turn the scone over and then place it back in the pan upside-down, cover with the remaining treacle batter mix and cook for a final 16 minutes. Serve to friends, family and villagers just like the old days.

STICKY TOFFEE ORKNEY BROONIE

SERVES 8

INGREDIENTS

For the broonie

2 eggs

175ml (¾ cup) buttermilk

65ml (¼ cup + 1 teaspoon) milk

125g (4½oz) butter

125g (4½oz) light brown sugar

75g (2½oz) black treacle

175g (6¼oz) plain flour

175g (6¼oz) porridge oats

1 teaspoon bicarbonate of soda

2½ tablespoons ground ginger

Pinch of salt

For the sauce

150g (5oz) butter

300g (10½oz) muscovado sugar

1 tablespoon black treacle

200ml (¾ cup + 1 tablespoon) double cream

I discovered this Orkney bake in F. Marian McNeill's 1929 cookbook *The Scots Kitchen*. Traditionally, an oat gingerbread baked as a classic loaf; I couldn't resist giving it my own twist. Here, I've transformed it into a scrumptious traybake, covered in a sticky toffee sauce, perfect for serving as a delectable dessert.

METHOD

To make the broonie

Preheat the oven to 150°C fan (340°F), grease and line a 20cm x 20cm (8" x 8") traybake tin.

In a bowl, whisk together the eggs, buttermilk and milk.

In a pan over a medium heat, melt together the butter, sugar and black treacle until combined and then stir in the porridge oats.

In another bowl, add all the other dry ingredients and mix in the eggy milk mixture, then the oaty treacle mixture and combine.

Pour the mixture into the tin and bake in the oven for 45 minutes or until a cocktail stick comes out clean.

To make the sauce

Meanwhile, add the butter, sugar and black treacle to a pan and simmer until the sugar has dissolved and the butter melted. Then turn up the heat and let it bubble for a minute or so to create a dark toffee-coloured sauce. Take it off the heat and stir in the cream.

As soon as the Broonie is out of the oven, prick the cooked sponge pudding all over with a cocktail stick and pour about a quarter of the warm sauce over it.

Serve warm with a slice of the Broonie covered in extra toffee sauce and a big scoop of vanilla ice cream.

CRANACHAN TRUFFLES

MAKES ABOUT 16

INGREDIENTS

150g (5oz) dark chocolate

225g (8oz) white chocolate

200ml (¾ cup +
    1 tablespoon) double
    cream

80g (2¾oz) butter

2 tablespoons honey

2 tablespoons Jura whisky

For decoration

Freeze-dried raspberries

Crushed oaty biscuits
    (HobNobs work
    perfectly!)

Inspired by the traditional Scottish dessert cranachan, these chocolate truffles bring together the rich indulgence of chocolate with the delightful flavours of honey, whisky, raspberries and oats.

To capture the essence of cranachan, the truffles are rolled in a mixture of oaty biscuits and dried raspberries. The crushed oaties provide a delightful crunch and nutty undertone, reminiscent of the traditional dessert's oat component. The dried raspberries add a burst of tartness and fruity sweetness, the perfect complement to the chocolate.

METHOD

Roughly chop the chocolates into 2 bowls – one white and one dark. Add the cream, butter and honey to a saucepan. Once it comes to a bubbling simmer, pour half over the white chocolate and half over the dark chocolate.

Whisk the chocolate mixtures until they start to thicken, then add a tablespoon of whisky into each bowl of chocolate.

Allow to cool, then place in the fridge to set for a minimum of 2 hours.

Scoop out small portions of the chilled chocolate mixture with a teaspoon, then roll them into balls with your hands.

Sprinkle the freeze-dried raspberries on one board and the crushed oaty biscuits on another board and roll half the balls in the raspberries and half in the biscuits until completely coated. Chill again until time to serve.

TREACLE SCONES

MAKES 6

INGREDIENTS

200g (7oz) self-raising flour

25g (1oz) sugar

50g (1¾oz) butter, cubed

½ teaspoon ground cinnamon

½ teaspoon mixed spice

½ teaspoon baking powder

60g (2oz) black treacle

125ml (½ cup) milk

Pinch of salt

This recipe brings the sweet, spicy flavours of gingerbread to this traditional Scottish scone. Baking these scones to perfection allows the treacle to caramelise and develop its rich flavour while creating a crisp exterior. These hearty scones evoke a sense of nostalgia and are best enjoyed fresh from the oven, when their warmth and indulgence are at their peak!

METHOD

Preheat the oven to 190°C fan (410°F). Sift the flour, sugar and salt into a bowl. Add the butter and, using your fingers, rub it in lightly until the mixture looks like fine breadcrumbs. Stir in the spices and baking powder.

Mix the black treacle and milk together in a cup. Pour most of the milk and treacle mixture into the dry mix and stir through – only add the rest of the liquid if required. You want a nice soft dough, but it shouldn't be too wet.

Leave the dough to rest for a few minutes to absorb the liquid thoroughly. Flour your work surface and rolling pin well, then tip out the rested dough and roll out it to a 3cm (1") thickness.

Cut the dough into fluted rounds with a cookie cutter and place on a baking tray.

Bake in the oven for 10 minutes, until well risen and golden brown. Transfer to a wire rack to cool. Serve while still slightly warm and spread with a little butter.

Am fear as fhaide a chaidh on taigh 's e an ceòl a bu bhinne a chuala e a-riamh thighinn dhachaigh.

THERE'S NO PLACE LIKE HOME.

ECCLEFECHAN TARTS

MAKES 6

INGREDIENTS

For the filling

60g (2oz) butter, melted

100g (3½oz) soft dark brown sugar

1 egg, beaten

1 tablespoon orange juice

3 tablespoons whisky

150g (5oz) mixed dried fruit

50g (1¾oz) walnuts, roughly chopped

1 orange, zested

For the pastry

200g (7oz) plain flour

65g (2¼oz) butter, cubed

75g (2½oz) sugar

1 orange, zested

1 large egg yolk

2½ tablespoons ice-cold water (you may need a little more)

The Gaelic name for the village of Ecclefechan in Dumfries and Galloway is *Eaglais Fhèichin*, with *eaglais* being the Gaelic word for church. Named after the village, Ecclefechan tarts are made with buttery pastry and a sweet filling of dried fruit, walnuts and orange flavours. The tarts are baked until the pastry turns golden and the filling caramelises, creating a heavenly aroma that fills the kitchen – perfect as a treat after a visit to church!

METHOD

To make the filling, add all the filling ingredients together into a bowl and set aside for an hour.

To make the pastry, rub together the flour and butter until it resembles fine breadcrumbs. Mix in the sugar and orange zest, then add the egg yolk and ice-cold water.

Bring together with your hands to form a dough. Sprinkle with a little more ice-cold water if the pastry is still too crumbly. Roll into a ball, wrap in clingfilm and chill in the fridge for 30 minutes.

Roll out the pastry on a lightly floured surface to 3mm (1⁄10″) thick. Use a fluted cookie cutter to stamp out circles of pastry. Press the pastry circles into the holes in a lightly greased tartlet tray and prick the bases with a fork. Place in the fridge for about 30 minutes.

Preheat the oven to 160°C fan (350°F).

Spoon the filling into the pastry cases and bake in the oven for 15 minutes until golden. Cool in their tins for 5 minutes, before carefully transferring to a wire rack.

TOASTED SELKIRK BANNOCK WITH MARMALADE SYRUP

SERVES 4

INGREDIENTS

For the bannock

250ml (1 cup) milk

100g (3½oz) butter

500g (1lb 2oz) strong white bread flour, plus extra for dusting

75g (2½oz) sugar

250g (9oz) sultanas

7g (¼oz) instant dried yeast

1 teaspoon salt

1 teaspoon oil, for greasing

For the marmalade syrup

80ml (⅓ cup) maple syrup

80g (2¾oz) marmalade

The first time we find the Selkirk Bannock written about is in Sir Walter Scott's novel *The Bride of Lammermoor*, which tells of a tragic love affair between young Lucy Ashton and her family's enemy Edgar Ravenswood. Soon after, Queen Victoria visited Scott's Abbotsford House. Much to her delight, in among the petticoat-tail shortbread and sweet scones at afternoon tea was the Selkirk Bannock. On her return south, she promptly instructed the royal kitchen staff to recreate these cherished treats.

To transform the Selkirk Bannock into a truly decadent delight, it is sliced and toasted until golden brown then generously drizzled with a luscious marmalade syrup. The syrup adds a zesty and slightly bittersweet note that beautifully complements the sweetness of the bread. It seeps into every nook and cranny, infusing the toast with a sticky and flavourful essence. Move over French toast, we have a Scottish rival to your crown!

METHOD

Pour the milk into a medium pan, add the butter, then heat gently until the butter has melted.

Put the flour, sugar, sultanas, yeast and salt in a bowl, keeping the yeast and salt separate. Pour in the milk mixture, then stir until you have a smooth dough.

Turn out onto a floured surface, knead for about 5 minutes and transfer to an oiled bowl. Cover and leave to rise in a warm place for an hour, or until doubled in size.

Now, knock back the dough on a floured surface, shape into a loaf and transfer to a greased baking tray.

Cover loosely with oiled clingfilm and leave to rise again for between 30 and 60 minutes.

Preheat the oven to 160°C fan (350°F) and bake the loaf for around 40 minutes, until it's golden and makes a hollow sound when you tap it on the bottom.

For the marmalade syrup, add the maple syrup and marmalade to a small saucepan and bring to a simmer, stirring constantly.

To serve, toast thick slices of the bannock on a grill pan, top with your syrup and perhaps a dollop of mascarpone.

WHISKY MACARONS

MAKES A DOZEN

INGREDIENTS

For the macarons

100g (3½oz) egg whites

100g (3½oz) sugar

100g (3½oz) ground almonds

100g (3½oz) icing sugar

30g (1oz) cocoa powder

Pinch of salt

For the ganache

225g (8oz) dark chocolate

225ml (¾ cup + 3 tablespoons) double cream

2 tablespoons whisky

1 teaspoon vanilla bean paste

Pinch of salt

Whisky macarons are the perfect fusion of French pastry finesse and Scottish spirit. These wee treats combine the delicate, airy texture of macarons with the rich, complex flavours of whisky. The chocolate ganache is infused with whisky, allowing the flavours to develop a luxurious taste. I love to use a 10-year-old Jura whisky. Oh, and pour yourself a dram – it's the chef's prerogative!

METHOD

To make the macarons

Line 2 baking sheets with baking parchment.

To a heatproof bowl, add the egg whites and 3 tablespoons of the sugar. Place the bowl over a pan of simmering hot water and whisk continuously until the sugar has melted and the egg whites become white and frothy, which should take about 1 minute, then remove from the heat.

Whisk in the rest of the sugar for another 3 to 4 minutes, until stiff meringue peaks form. Next, sift together the ground almonds, icing sugar, cocoa powder and salt, then fold into your meringues carefully.

Transfer the batter to a piping bag fitted with a large round nozzle. Hold the bag vertically to the tray, with the nozzle about 1cm (½") from it. Pipe rounds about 2½cm (1") in diameter onto the prepared baking sheets. Use a wet fingertip to tap down any tips left on top of the macarons. Leave to rest for 30 minutes, or until the macarons have developed a skin.

Preheat the oven to 150°C fan (340°F). Place your macarons in for 13 minutes, then allow to cool completely before removing from the baking sheets.

To make the ganache

Break up the chocolate, add half to a bowl and place in the microwave in bursts of 20 seconds until melted, then add the rest of the chocolate and stir until completely melted. Meanwhile, add your double cream to a pan and heat until it simmers.

Pour the cream over the melted chocolate and leave for 2 minutes, then begin to stir with a whisk until you get a creamy consistency. Add the whisky, vanilla and salt; whisk until combined and leave to set until thickened. Place the ganache into a piping bag and pipe on half the macarons and sandwich the rest on top. Et voilà!

THE FAIRY FLAG

When Harald Hardrada, the eleventh-century Norwegian king, returned from a battle in the Mediterranean with a piece of Persian silk, little did he know he would change Scottish folklore and the Clan MacLeod family history for ever. But he did . . .

On his return, he asked his wife Princess Elisiv of Kyiv to turn the silk into a battle flag, which he named Landetðuna. It didn't bring Harald much luck, though. The flag flew over him when he was killed fighting the English at the Battle of Stamford Bridge in 1066. One of the few Viking survivors of that battle was Godred Crovan, a Norse-Gael ruler of the Kingdom of the Isles. Godred fled from Yorkshire to the Hebrides, taking the battle flag with him, where he joined his sister Helga of the Beautiful Hair.

As Godred began to win more and more battles flying the Landetðuna flag, rumours began to spread throughout the islands that the flag was imbued with magical powers. But, with Godred's death on Islay in 1095, the whereabouts of his battle flag became a mystery.

A century later, the Chieftain of the MacLeods was walking up Sgurr na Banachdaich when suddenly a beautiful, graceful woman appeared by the waterfall on the Allt a' Choire Ghreadaidh. Her name was Àine, and the Chieftain fell in love with her immediately. However, on the night when the Chieftain sought her hand in marriage, she confessed to him her true identity as a Fairy Princess, one belonging to a realm beyond this world.

The Chieftain had been brought up to fear the *ban-sìthe*. He had been told that the faeries had stolen away children, brought illness and destroyed crops. But he could not stop himself loving Àine and they begged her father, the Fairy King, to let them get married. At first he refused, saying it would break his daughter's heart as her husband would grow old and die, while she would live for ever. Moved by her tears, the King eventually agreed but on one condition: at the end of a year and a day she must return for ever to the otherworld.

The couple cherished their magnificent wedding ceremony, and within a year, they were blessed with a beautiful son. Alas, the year and a day passed too quickly, and it was time for the Fairy Princess to keep her promise and return to her father, the Fairy King, who was waiting for her on the bridge that is now known as 'The Fairy Bridge'.

Before she left, the Fairy Princess hugged her son and husband for the last time and made the Chieftain promise that he would never allow their young son to be left alone and to cry, for she would hear his cries, even far away in the fairy kingdom under the hills.

The Chieftain of the MacLeods was heartbroken after his beautiful wife left, and his grief only deepened with time. He returned every day to the waterfall on the Allt a' Choire Ghreadaidh hoping to catch a glimpse of her again. In an attempt to lift his spirits, the household staff at Dunvegan Castle orchestrated a grand birthday feast for the Chieftain, filled with singing, dancing, piping and harping. Before long, he found himself immersed in the joyous atmosphere, relishing the celebration.

There was so much music and laughter that the baby's nursemaid slipped out of the nursery to watch the fun from the top of the stairs. The baby boy awoke and began to cry. The nursemaid, though, did not hear him and he was left to cry pitifully, all alone.

Upon the nursemaid's return, she was surprised to see a tall and slender woman, with long flowing hair and piercing blue eyes, wrapping the baby in a silk shawl and singing softly to him. The nursemaid was mesmerised and stood by the door listening to the tune. When the baby stopped crying, the woman put him gently back into his cradle, kissed him and vanished into the night.

The nursemaid never told anyone about what she had seen that night. She knew she shouldn't have left the bed chamber and was afraid that no one would believe her, or that they would think she was insane. But she always swaddled the baby in the silk shawl left by the beautiful woman, knowing it never failed to soothe his tears.

When the Chieftain's son turned ten, he told his father of the night his mother visited him. He said that she told him that the shawl was magic and could be used by the MacLeods in times of great danger to summon the fairy army to their side. But his mother had also warned him that the flag could only be used three times. The Chieftain knew immediately that Àine had returned to watch over their son. He ordered a special casket to be made to hold the Fairy Flag and he carried it with him at all times.

Years later, there came a time of great danger. The Clan MacDonald launched a devastating raid on the island. On a fateful Sunday, they mercilessly attacked the MacLeods' church, setting it ablaze and claiming the lives of the innocent worshippers within.

Left with dwindling numbers and hopelessly outnumbered, the MacLeods gathered on the sandy shores, their spirits aflame with vengeance. In a moment of desperation, they unfurled the legendary Fairy Flag. Miraculously, the humble band appeared to multiply tenfold, as if touched by ethereal forces. Their adversaries, the MacDonalds, stricken with terror, swiftly turned tail and fled.

A decade passed and a devastating famine descended upon the islands, leaving a trail of death and despair. Cattle and sheep succumbed to the harsh conditions, lying lifeless and on the brink of death. With the spectre of starvation looming over the MacLeod clan, the Chieftain turned to their last glimmer of hope – the enchanted flag.

With solemn determination, they unfurled the flag once again, invoking the aid of the mystical fairy host. In a mesmerising display, the ethereal riders emerged and touched the ailing animals with their enchanted swords. In an instant, a miraculous transformation occurred, as the once feeble creatures regained their vitality and health. The clan, saved from the clutches of hunger, rejoiced at this extraordinary intervention, forever indebted to the mystical powers of the flag.

Nowadays, it might look like a faded, battered bit of cloth with a few strange markings, but this is the famous Fairy Flag that is kept safely at Dunvegan Castle on the Isle of Skye.

The flag has yet to be used for a third time and still has a single miracle left to give. During the Second World War, there were rumours that when the looming threat of invasion cast a shadow over the nation, the Clan Chief offered to transport the flag to unfurl over the white cliffs of Dover. The intention behind this gesture was to harness the flag's reputed protective powers in defence of the nation.

Winston Churchill's reaction to this offer remains unknown. Whether he considered it a genuine possibility or regarded it as a folklore-inspired gesture is a matter of speculation, lost to the annals of history. Nonetheless, the offer itself stands as a testament to the enduring belief and allegiance of the Clan MacLeod to the legend of the Fairy Flag.

So, are the Landetðuna flag brought back to the island by Godred Crovan and the Fairy Flag gifted to the Chieftain's son by Àine one and the same? That we will never know. But that tune sung by the Fairy Princess to her child that evening? Well known as 'The Cradle Spell of Dunvegan', it is still being sung on the island to this day.

THE CRADLE SPELL OF DUNVEGAN

Sleep, my little child, Hero tenderling,
Dream, my little child, Hero fawnlike one,
High on mountain brows, Be thy stagtryst,
Speed thy yew arrows straight antlerwards.

Sleep, my little child, Hero gentle bred,
Dream, my little child, Hero battle bred,
Skin like falling snow, Green thy mailcoat,
Live thy steeds, Dauntless thy following.

Horo i la o, Horo a li e,
Horo i la o, Horo a li e,
Dream thy hero dream, Through thy child sleep,
Hang thy shield, Lochlann-like, heavenwards.

BEETROOT SOUP

SERVES 6

INGREDIENTS

1 tablespoon vegetable oil

1 onion, chopped

2 sticks celery, diced

3 beetroots, diced (keep the stalks and leaves)

1 carrot, diced

1 potato, diced

2 garlic cloves, finely chopped

1½ litre (1 quart + 2 cups) beef or vegetable stock

½ green cabbage, finely shredded

2 tomatoes, chopped

To serve

Soured cream and fresh dill, or crumbled feta cheese

From Borscht to Chlodnik, Ciorbă de Sfeclăto to Shorba Alassal, beetroot soups are loved around the world. And, luckily, beetroots grow really well in Scottish vegetable plots, especially ours! This vibrant and nourishing soup celebrates the beetroot's earthy flavours and vibrant colour. And, once you've made it, it's a recipe you'll keep returning to time and again.

METHOD

Heat the oil in a large pan. Sauté the onion and celery for 5 minutes, then add the beetroot, carrot, potato and garlic, then sauté for a couple more minutes. Add the stock and season well and simmer for 15 minutes.

Add the cabbage and tomatoes and allow to simmer for another 20 minutes. Chop the stalks and leaves of the beetroot and, just before serving, stir into the soup and allow them to warm through.

Serve with a dollop of soured cream, a sprinkling of dill or topped with crumbled feta cheese.

SHALLOT TARTE TATIN

SERVES 4

INGREDIENTS

320g (11¼oz) pack of ready-rolled puff pastry

1 tablespoon olive oil

400g (14oz) banana shallots, peeled and halved

50g (1¾oz) sugar

2 tablespoons balsamic vinegar

2 tablespoons sherry vinegar

1 tablespoon butter

A few sprigs thyme, leaves picked

This one is definitely for Peter. He has been asking me to recreate a dish similar to one we had in a restaurant last year, which he talked about for months (and months) afterwards! After countless attempts and fine-tuning, he finally declared this as close to perfect as it's possible to get. With its golden, caramelised shallots nestled in a flaky puff pastry crust, whether served as an appetiser, side dish, or the star of a vegetarian feast, it's sure to impress your guests.

METHOD

Roll out the puff pastry to a 5mm (⅕") thickness, then cut it into a circle measuring about 2½cm (1") larger in diameter than the large ovenproof frying pan (about 27½cm; 11") you'll be making the tarte in. Transfer the pastry circle to a lined baking tray and chill for about 20 minutes.

Heat the oven to 160°C fan (350°F).

Heat the olive oil in the frying pan. Fry the shallot halves for 4 to 5 minutes until caramelised. Add the sugar and vinegars, and cook for 10 minutes, turning and basting the shallots regularly. Once the shallots are tender, stir in the butter and thyme, and arrange neatly, with the cut sides facing down, cooling slightly.

Put the pastry circle over the shallots, tucking it down and round at the edges and prick a few times with a knife to allow steam to escape. Bake in the oven for 25 minutes until puffed and golden brown.

Cool for 5 minutes, then put a large serving plate over the pan and very carefully flip it over to turn the tart out.

RHUBARB CHUTNEY

MAKES 3 JARS

INGREDIENTS

800g (1¾lb) rhubarb, trimmed and cut into 3cm (1¼") chunks

2 red onions, finely sliced

200g (7oz) light brown soft sugar

200ml (¾ cup + 1 tablespoon) cider vinegar

50g (1¾oz) sultanas

1 star anise

1 small cinnamon stick

10 black peppercorns

3 bay leaves

If you find yourself with a glut of rhubarb from your garden and can only manage to eat rhubarb crumble twice a day (a dream day in my opinion!), it's great to have another recipe to use up your seasonal bounty. Whether paired with cheese, spread on sandwiches, or served alongside cold meats, this vibrant chutney adds a real burst of flavour. Perfect to gift to friends and family, too.

METHOD

Put half the rhubarb in a heavy-based pan with all the other ingredients. Simmer over a medium/high heat for 20 minutes, stirring occasionally, until all the liquid has evaporated and the relish is thick and jammy. The rhubarb will break down completely. Remove the whole spices.

Stir in the remaining rhubarb, reduce the heat to a low simmer and cook for a further 7 minutes, stirring frequently, until the new batch of rhubarb is soft but retains its shape. Cool completely and transfer to sterilised jars; your chutney will then keep for up to 3 months.

An uair a 's mò 'n èiginn, dearbhar an caraid dìleas.

A FRIEND IN NEED IS A FRIEND INDEED.

HIGHLAND TARTIFLETTE

SERVES 4

INGREDIENTS

1kg (2lb 3oz) potatoes

160g (5½oz) smoked pancetta

2 onions, sliced

1 garlic clove, peeled and finely chopped

125ml (½ cup) white wine

250ml (1 cup) double cream

240g (8½oz) Minger cheese

Black pepper, to season

Olive oil, for frying

The comfort food of kings! Hailing from the French Alps, this classic dish combines layers of creamy potatoes, onions, smoky bacon and gooey Reblochon cheese. To make this with a Scottish twist, I recommend using Minger cheese from Highland Fine Cheeses at Blarliath Farm in Tain. Hearty and flavoursome, this is the perfect dish to serve after a day climbing a Munro or two!

METHOD

Peel and chop your potatoes into 2 to 3cm (¾ to 1") chunks, place in a pan of water and simmer for 10 minutes, or until nearly cooked. Drain and set aside.

In a large ovenproof frying pan, fry the pancetta in olive oil. Add the onions and cook gently for about 10 to 15 minutes, until the onions are soft and golden. Add the garlic for the final minute.

Increase the heat and add the wine, let it bubble away until evaporated, then add in the chopped potatoes. Cook, stirring often, for a couple of minutes, until the potatoes are just lightly browned. Add the cream, stir and cook for 2 minutes. Season with freshly ground black pepper.

Preheat the oven to 180°C fan (400°F).

Remove the pan from the heat, slice the cheese and stir half in with the potatoes. Top the pan with the remaining sliced cheese, rind side showing, and pop into the oven for 10 to 15 minutes, until golden and bubbling.

Serve immediately and start planning which Munro you're going to conquer next!

LEEK BREAD & BUTTER PUDDING

SERVES 4 TO 6

INGREDIENTS

2 leeks

30g (1oz) butter

1 tablespoon Dijon mustard

Sourdough loaf, 8 slices

4 eggs

500ml (2 cups) milk

200g (7oz) Isle of Arran Blue Cheese, broken into small chunks

200g (7oz) Cheddar cheese, grated

Oil, for frying

As the chill of autumn sets in, there's nothing quite as comforting as this vegetarian lunch dish. This quick, hearty recipe, flavoured with leeks and cheese, is just as good, if not better, than its sweet counterpart. Just don't tell that to my Marmalade Bread & Butter Pudding recipe from my first book! You can use up stale bread for this recipe; it'll soak up the flavours even better.

METHOD

Chop your leeks, add them to some oil in a frying pan, then cook gently for 6 to 8 minutes over a low heat.

Meanwhile, stir together the butter and the mustard and thinly spread on one side of each slice of your sourdough bread. Cut each slice into two triangles.

In a large jug, beat the eggs and milk and season well.

Preheat the oven to 170°C fan (375°F). Arrange your sourdough triangles in a pattern of pointy side up, pointy side down in your oven dish. Scatter with a third of the leeks and a third of the cheeses, then pour over a third of the milk mixture, evenly and slowly. Repeat to use up the remaining ingredients, then leave to soak for 20 minutes.

Place the dish on a baking sheet and cook for 30 to 40 minutes, until risen and golden. Serve immediately.

SPICED CARROT HOT CROSS BUNS

MAKES A DOZEN

INGREDIENTS

For the buns

300ml (1¼ cup) milk

50g (1¾oz) butter

500g (1lb 2oz) strong bread flour, plus extra for dusting

75g (2½oz) sugar

7g (¼oz) sachet fast-action dried yeast

1 teaspoon salt

1 teaspoon ground cinnamon

½ teaspoon freshly ground nutmeg

1 egg, beaten

80g (2¾oz) carrots

100g (3½oz) raisins

A little oil, for rising the dough

For the crosses

100g (3½oz) plain flour

4 tablespoons water

To glaze

2 tablespoons apricot jam

Picture this: soft and fluffy buns infused with the sweet, earthy flavours of carrots and generously spiced with cinnamon and nutmeg. Can you already smell the amazing aroma wafting from your oven? These are classic Easter treats, but without the cross these would grace your table at any time of year.

METHOD

To make the buns

In a pan, heat the milk gently until it begins to simmer. Add the butter and leave it to cool slightly.

Add the flour, sugar, yeast, salt and spices to a large bowl.

When the milk has cooled to lukewarm, make a well in the centre of the flour mixture, pour the milk in and add the beaten egg.

Mix well with a wooden spoon, then use your hands to bring everything together into a sticky dough.

On a lightly floured work surface knead the dough until it's smooth, which should take about 10 minutes.

Lightly oil a bowl and add the dough. Cover the bowl with oiled clingfilm and leave to rise in a warm place for an hour or until doubled in size.

Peel and grate the carrot, then wring it out in a clean tea towel to remove excess moisture. Add it to the bowl of dough along with the raisins. Knead the dough in the bowl to evenly distribute.

Divide the dough into 12 equal-sized pieces and shape into small round buns. Place them onto a baking tray, leaving room for them to expand, and cover with oiled clingfilm. Leave to rise again for an hour.

Heat the oven to 180°C fan (400°F) and line a baking tray.

To make the crosses

In a bowl, mix the flour with the water to make a thick paste. Spoon into a piping bag and, with a small nozzle, pipe a line along each row of buns, then repeat in the other direction to create crosses.

Bake for 20 minutes or until golden brown then transfer to a wire rack.

Heat the apricot jam, then use a pastry brush to brush it onto the tops of the warm buns and allow to cool.

APPLE VICTORIA

SERVES 6

INGREDIENTS

For the sponge

340g (12oz) butter

340g (12oz) sugar

340g (12oz) self-raising flour

1½ teaspoons baking powder

6 eggs

3 eating apples, Braeburn or Pink Lady are my favourites, or of course ones from my very own apple tree!

Icing sugar, for dusting

For the cinnamon buttercream

270g (9½oz) slightly salted butter, softened

500g (1lb 2oz) icing sugar

2 teaspoons ground cinnamon

1 teaspoon mixed spice

3½ teaspoons milk

1 teaspoon vanilla bean paste

After planting six apple trees a couple of years ago, I am already preparing for a harvest of apples this autumn! An undeniable classic, a Victoria sponge is one of the simplest cakes there is and definitely one of the tastiest. The addition of grated apple adds a burst of flavour and makes the cake extra moist. I've added layers of luscious cinnamon buttercream between the sponges that make for the perfect flavour combination.

METHOD

Preheat the oven to 160°C fan (350°F). Grease and line three 20cm (8") sandwich tins.

Measure all the sponge ingredients except the apple into a large bowl and combine. Peel and grate the apples, fold into the mixture, then divide between the tins and level the tops.

Bake in the oven for about 25 minutes until golden or until a skewer comes out clean.

Cool the cakes in the tins for 10 minutes, then place onto a wire rack.

To make the cinnamon buttercream

Put the butter in a large bowl and whisk until pale and creamy.

Sift in the icing sugar along with the cinnamon and mixed spice, then add the milk and vanilla, and beat until very pale and fluffy.

Sit one cake upside down on a serving plate. Spread the cinnamon buttercream to the edge of the sponge, place another gently on top to sandwich the cakes together and repeat.

Dust the top with icing sugar to serve.

COURGETTE & ELDERFLOWER CAKE

INGREDIENTS

For the cake

250g (9oz) butter

250g (9oz) golden caster
sugar

1 teaspoon vanilla bean
paste

½ a lemon, zested and juiced

2 tablespoons elderflower
cordial

300g (10½oz) plain flour

2 teaspoons baking powder

5 large eggs

150g (5oz) courgettes, grated

Pinch of salt

For the topping

200g (7oz) butter, softened

350g (12½oz) icing sugar,
sifted

2 tablespoons elderflower
cordial

75g (2½oz) unsalted
pistachio kernels

Take a slice of this and you'll get the floral essence of elderflower cordial and the subtle freshness of courgette in the most moist and irresistible cake. For the best results, opt for smaller courgettes, as they bring just the right amount of moisture to the cake. However, if you only have larger courgettes on hand, simply remove the seedy core before grating. This is the perfect cake to serve on a summer's day out in the garden.

METHOD

Preheat the oven to 140°C fan (325°F). Grease and line a 20cm (8″) round cake tin.

Cream the butter and sugar together until light and fluffy. Beat in the vanilla, lemon zest and juice, and the elderflower cordial. Sift the flour, baking powder and a pinch of salt into another bowl. Beat the eggs into the creamed mixture, one by one, adding a spoonful of the flour each time to stop it from curdling, then mix in the rest of the flour.

Fold in the grated courgette, then place your cake batter in the tin and bake for 1 hour 10 minutes or until a skewer comes out clean.

Cool the cake in the tin for 10 minutes, then place onto a wire rack.

For the elderflower buttercream icing, beat the butter then add half the icing sugar. Beat until smooth, then add the rest of the icing sugar along with the elderflower cordial, and beat to combine. Smooth your icing over the cooled cake, then finely chop the pistachios and use these to decorate.

RASPBERRY RIPPLE COOKIES

MAKES 18

INGREDIENTS

270g (9½oz) plain flour

¾ teaspoon bicarbonate of soda

160g (5½oz) butter

100g (3½oz) light brown sugar

100g (3½oz) sugar

1 egg

½ tablespoon vanilla bean paste

60g (2oz) white chocolate, chopped

60g (2oz) raspberries, chopped

Pinch of salt

Scotland is known for having the perfect conditions for growing raspberries. Long summer days with lots of light, but not too hot. Too much sun, and the fruits will ripen too quickly, losing some of the depth of flavour that develops with slower ripening.

With their beautiful swirls of raspberry goodness and a melt-in-your-mouth buttery texture – these cookies are the perfect treat. The combination of the tart raspberries and the sweet white chocolate is simply irresistible.

METHOD

Preheat the oven to 160°C fan (350°F) and prepare your baking sheets.

Add the flour, bicarbonate of soda and salt to a bowl and set it aside.

In another bowl, cream the butter and sugars together for 2 minutes until light and fluffy.

Mix in the egg and vanilla. Then combine with the dry ingredients, and fold in the white chocolate.

Gently fold the raspberries into the dough, then use your hands to form the dough into balls the size of one heaped teaspoon. Place these onto your baking sheet, allowing space between each one.

Bake for 10 minutes or until the edges are slightly golden brown and the middles look set. Let the cookies cool on the baking sheet for 10 minutes then transfer them to a wire rack to cool completely.

STRAWBERRY BUCKLE

INGREDIENTS

For the cake

85g (3oz) butter

150g (5oz) sugar

2 eggs

1 teaspoon vanilla bean paste

260g (9oz) plain flour

1½ teaspoons baking powder

½ teaspoon cinnamon

120ml (½ cup) milk

375g (13¼oz) strawberries

Pinch of salt

For the streusel topping

60g (2oz) butter

50g (1¾oz) sugar

55g (2oz) light brown sugar

45g (1½oz) plain flour

1 teaspoon cinnamon

Pinch of salt

Buckles are so named because the cake portion falls, or buckles, around the fruit during baking. This strawberry buckle has a moist, soft and fluffy cake, succulent ripe strawberries and a delectable cinnamon streusel topping. So, if you're in search of a sweet brunch dish that captures the essence of summer, look no further.

METHOD

Preheat oven to 160°C fan (350°F).

Cream the butter and sugar together until light and fluffy. Mix in the eggs and vanilla until well combined.

Into a bowl, sieve the flour, baking powder, salt and cinnamon. Add half the flour mixture until just combined, followed by the milk and then the remaining flour mixture.

Fold in half the strawberries. Pour the batter into a greased pie dish and top with the remaining strawberries.

To make the streusel topping, melt the butter in a pan and allow to cool a little. Combine all the other streusel ingredients in a bowl, pour over the melted butter, mix with a fork until well combined and sprinkle over the strawberries on top of the cake mix.

Bake for 45 minutes until lightly browned and until a skewer comes out mostly clean. Serve warm with cream or ice cream.

ÒRAN MÒR

It was in the summer of 1829 when Felix Mendelssohn first travelled to Scotland with his childhood friend, Carl Klingemann. After a few days in Edinburgh, of which he bluntly wrote 'looked so stern and robust, half enveloped in a haze of fog', he ventured west and took the boat to the Isle of Mull. It was here that his spirits lifted, and it was on his return from the island of Staffa that he wrote to his sister Fanny, 'In order to make you understand how extraordinarily the Hebrides affected me, I send you the following, which came into my head there.' The opening line of what would become 'The Hebrides' overture was scribbled at the top of the page.

His travel companion Klingemann described Fingal's Cave on Staffa saying, 'A greener rush of waves surely never rushed into a stranger cavern – its many pillars making it look like the inside of an immense organ, black and resounding, absolutely without purpose, and quite alone, the wide grey sea within and without.'

Klingemann's poetic descriptions capture the essence of Fingal's Cave, a place where the natural world and his friend's musical inspiration converged. Mendelssohn was deeply moved by the experience of standing within the cave, leading him to translate the awe and beauty he witnessed into the powerful musical language of his 'The Hebrides' overture.

Scottish islanders, and particularly the Gaels, are a people with a life steeped in music. With poetry and balladry as the beating heart of Gaelic tradition, our music is extremely rich in folklore and has been part of our everyday life for centuries. From waulking songs to lullabies, love songs to tragedies, songs of the sea to puirt-à-beul. All of which keep the stories, history and people of the islands alive with us today.

Wherever I am in the world, there are many Gaelic songs that evoke wonderful memories of family occasions, cèilidhs and performing at the Mòd. When Peter and I won the duet competition at the Royal National Mòd in 2018, we sang 'Tàladh na Beinne Guirme'. The first time I heard it was at the CCA in Glasgow at an event called Ceòl is Craic. Brian Ó hEadhra was performing and I was in awe of his voice and this tune.

Written by Brian and Goiridh mac Alasdair Dhùghaill of Cape Breton, it tells its story from the perspective of A' Bheinn Ghorm, the Blue Mountain. The mountain tells of the arrival of the Gaels to Nova Scotia and how it grew to love the people, their language and song. But then it laments the loss of their culture through the generations. In the final lines, the mountain promises to never stop singing the Gaelic songs it has learned in honour of the Gaels laid to rest around its foothills.

TÀLADH NA BEINNE GUIRME

Fàil ill ó 's ah ó ro éileadh o ro
Fàil ill é 's ah ó ro éileadh ó
Hiùrabh ó 's ah ó ro éileadh o ro
Fàil ill é 's ah ó ro éileadh ó.

A dhaoine, bha mi 'seo bho'n a bhris an là,
Sìnte, gu sìtheil 'na mo shuain,
'S an t-sìorraidheachd, am bòidhchead slàn mar a
    dheònaich E,
'S an nàdar a' freagairt dha mo dhuan.

Air maduinn, dh'fhairich mi ann dealachadh,
Mo chaithris is m'ònrachd 'tighinn gu ceann,
Ceòl na tuaighe is nan duanagan,
Dh'èist mi is thog mi fhìn am fonn.

Daoine, daoine còire, curanta,
A ghiùlain gach cruadal 's càs gu treun,
Dualchas, dualchas beairteach, breagha, beò,
Mar chàirdean, gun d' thug iad orm seinn.

Ach thàinig, thàinig oirnn an dàrna là,
Is chunnaic mi mo dhaltan a' sìoladh às,
'S gann gun cluinn mi an cànan ceòlmhor, blasda,
    binn,
Cànan coimheach, cruaidh a' tighinn na h-àit'.

Tha sgleò, tha sgleò air tighinn air an àite seo,
Is sàmhchair bhon a dh'fhalbh móran,
'Nam chaithris air mo chloinn nan cadal buan,
Fanaidh mi 'gan tàladh ann lem òran.

THE LULLABY OF THE BLUE MOUNTAIN

Fàil ill ó 's ah ó ro éileadh o ro
Fàil ill é 's ah ó ro éileadh ó
Hiùrabh ó 's ah ó ro éileadh o ro
Fàil ill é 's ah ó ro éileadh ó.

O people, I was here since the dawning of the first
    day,
Reclining, peacefully in my slumber,
In eternity, in total beauty as He willed it,
And nature suiting and replying to my song.

In the morning, I sensed a change,
My watching and my solitude coming to an end,
The music of the axe and of songs,
I listened and I joined in with their chorus.

People, a kind and dauntless people,
Who bravely endured every hardship and distress,
A culture, a rich, beautiful, living culture,
As friends, they caused me to sing.

But great change overtook us,
And I saw my foster-children dying out,
Rarely do I hear the melodious, sweet language,
There's a foreign, hard-sounding language in its
    stead.

A pall has come upon this place,
And silence, since so many have departed,
I am wakeful and watchful over my children in their
    eternal slumber,
I will remain, lullabying them with my song.

Village bards known as *Bàird Bhaile* were important figures in Gaelic society for centuries. They were commissioned to compose songs, both solemn and satirical, for the Clan Chiefs and to perform at the local cèilidhs.

It is believed that *Bàird Bhaile* were almost always men, as composing poetry was not considered an appropriate profession for women at the time. Though some records of female village bards do appear.

Màiri nighean Alasdair Ruaidh, Mary MacLeod, was a seventeenth-century bard who composed poems of praise about the heroic adventures of the MacLeods and their Chief. She began composing poems while working as a nurse for the MacLeod family, but was later exiled to Mull after writing one particular poem.

The story goes, the Clan Chief of MacLeod was displeased with her poem written about his cousin, Sir Norman Macleod of Bernera, as he felt it praised him too highly and so he banished Mary from the island. He eventually allowed her to return on the condition that she couldn't compose anymore. In public, she agreed, but this didn't stop Mary and, in secret, she continued to write her poems and songs until she found her final resting place at St Clement's Church in the village of Rodel on the Isle of Harris.

In the song 'Thèid mi lem Dheòin', she tells of how she can finally go back to Dunvegan, and that the exile from the MacLeod family is over.

THÈID MI LEM DHEÒIN

Thèid mi lem dheòin do dhùthaich MhicLeòid,
M'iùil air a' phòr luath-lamhach;
Bu chòir dhomh gum bi m' eòlas san tìr
Leòdach mur pill cruadal mi.

Siubhlaidh mi an iar fo dhùbhlach nan sian
Don tùr g'am beil triall thuath-cheatharn,
On chualas an sgeul buadhach gun bhreug
Rinn acain mo chlèibh fhuadachadh.

Iomairt gu leòr mar ri MacLeòid,
Bàta fo sheòl uain-dhathte,
Bho àras an fhìon gu talla nam pìos,
'S gum beannaich an Rìgh 'n t-uasal sin.

Seinnidh mi ceòl air cinneadh MhicLeòid
'S air ionad nan sròl luaineach ud,
Innis nam bàrd cinneadail gràidh,
Duineil ri dàimh dualachais.

Tormodach fial shliochd Olghair nan sgiath,
Foirmeil do thriall uarach-sa;
Deàlradh nam pìos, torman nam pìob
'S mi dearbhte gur leibh dualachas.

Thèid mise dham dheòin Dhùn Bheagain nan còrn,
Far am faighte ann an tòs Màighe mi,
Gu talla nan cliar far am faramach fìon
'S gum beannaicheadh Dia an t-àras-sa.

I WILL GLADLY GO

I will gladly go to the land of MacLeod,
steering my course towards the ready-handed kin.
It is right that I will know my way,
unless hardship drives me back.

I will travel from the west under the storms,
to the tower to which tenantry resort,
since I have heard the news, precious and true,
which has banished the pang in my breast.

Bustle in plenty is found with MacLeod,
a boat under green-coloured sail,
from the house of wine to the hall of goblets,
and may the King bless that nobleman.

I will sing a song about MacLeod's clan
and about that place of waving satin banners,
the refuge of poets, clannish and loving,
hospitable to long-established friends.

Generous descendant of Tormod from the kin of
    Olghar of the shields,
your regular ceremonials are stately:
with the gleaming of the goblets and the roar of
    the pipes
I am certain that you have a great inheritance.

I will gladly go to Dunvegan of the drinking-horns,
where I used to be found at the beginning of May:
to the hall of the poet-bands where wine flows
    noisily,
and may God bless this dwelling.

One of Glen Orchy's most famous sons, the Gaelic bard, Duncan Ban MacIntyre was a key figure in the eighteenth-century Scottish Gaelic literary revival. MacIntyre's poetry is known for its beauty, humour, vivid imagery and reflections on life. His poems often explored themes of love, loss, nature and drinking!

Given the islanders' love of whisky, it is surprising that there are so few traditional Gaelic songs that celebrate their enormous capacity for drinking.

When I was selecting my songs to perform at the Royal National Mòd's Silver Pendant competition in 2017, I visited the Gaelic poet, composer and singer Sandy NicDhòmhnaill Jones. It was Sandy who shared Duncan Ban's song 'Òran a Bhotail' with me and, the moment we began singing it together, I knew I wanted to perform it on the Mòd stage.

'Òran a Bhotail' is a popular song by Duncan Ban that showcases his wit, conviviality and merriment. It celebrates not only drink, but also the prowess of those who indulge in it. And when it won me the Silver Pendant that year in Lochaber, I definitely celebrated with a few drams!

ÒRAN A BHOTAIL

Nuair shuidheas sinn socair 's a dh'òlas sinn botal,
chan aithnich ar stoc bhuainn na chuireas sinn ann;
thig onair is fortan le solas a' chopain:
carson nach biodh deoch oirnn mun tog sinn ar
    ceann?

Bheir an stuth grinn oirnn sein gu fileanta,
chuir a thoil-inntinn binneas nar cainnt;
chaisg i ar n-iota, an fhior dheoch mhilis:
bu mhuladach sinne nam biodh i air chall!

Deoch-slàinte nan gaisgeach, nan Gàidhealaibh
    gasta,
dham b' abhaist mar fhasan bhith poit air an dram:
luchd gaoil an stuth bhlasta, s' air dhaoiread an
    lacha,
nach caomhnach am beairteas a sgapadh san am.

Am fear ga bheil nì, gheibh e na shireas e,
'm fear a tha crionta, fanadh e thall;
am fear a tha miothair chan fhuiling sinn idir,
's am fear ga bheil grinneas thèid iomain a-nall.

On shuidh sinn cho fada 's a dh'òl sinn na bh'
    againn,
's i chòir dol a chadal on thàinig an t-àm;
chan fhòghnadh ach pailteas thoirt solas dhar
    n-aigne,
deoch mhòr anns a' mhadainn gu leigheas ar
    ceann.

Am fear tha gun chli, cuiridh e spiorad ann,
togaidh e cridhe gach fir a tha fann;
theid am fear tinn gu grinn air mhire:
's e leigheas gach tinneis, deoch mhilis an dram.

SONG OF THE BOTTLE

When canty we settle and finish a bottle,
We'll ne'er miss the total, whatever we pay;
Us honour and fortune in luck's glass importune,
Then why not be tipsy ere we go away?

The fine stuff will make us to singing betake us,
Its pleasure did wake us to song in our toast:
Our thirst it has drowned, the truly sweet round,
We were mourners profound if it should be lost.

A health to the wale of kind heroes, the Gael,
Themselves wont to regale, drinking drams to the
    end:
Were the bill ne'er so tough, lovers of the good stuff
Would not spare wealth enough opportunely to
    spend.

A man who has plenty will get what he'll want aye,
The saving and scanty let him bide outby.
The man who is near we will not suffer here,
But the kind man and dear, quickly let him come
    nigh.

We've long the seat pressed, and drunk all we
    possessed,
Go to sleep it were best since come round has the
    time;
Save plenty serves no less our nature to solace,
To make our heads' woe less comes the morn's
    draught sublime.

Whoe'er has no pith, it will him supply with,
it all hearts uplifteth that in sicknesses sink,
sick men will proceed finely to mirth indeed;
For all illness remede is the sweet dram of drink.

So, it wasn't just Mendelssohn who the Hebrides inspired to write a song; many before and still now are inspired by the landscapes, people and stories of the islands. Long may it continue!

If you're now inspired to listen to some Gaelic songs, turn to page 241 where I have compiled a playlist of songs and wonderful musicians to listen to while you're baking. Enjoy!

JAMMY DODGERS

MAKES A DOZEN

INGREDIENTS

115g (4oz) butter

115g (4oz) sugar

1 egg, beaten

½ teaspoon vanilla bean paste

250g (9oz) plain flour, plus extra for dusting

2 tablespoons raspberry jam

2 tablespoons lemon curd

Welcome to the delightful world of scrumptious homemade treats! Jammy dodgers are a classic for a reason, with their 2 layers of buttery shortbread filled with jam, traditionally raspberry, but also delicious with lemon curd. Jammy dodgers are the perfect treat to make with kids, and they are sure to be gone in no time. In fact, you may want to make a double batch!

METHOD

Cream the butter and sugar in a bowl until light and fluffy. Slowly beat in the egg and vanilla.

Sift in the flour and mix to a crumbly dough. Knead on a lightly floured surface until smooth; if the dough is a bit sticky, add a wee bit more flour. Shape the dough into a flat disc, wrap in clingfilm and chill in the fridge for 45 minutes.

Roll the chilled dough out on a lightly floured surface to a 3mm (¹⁄₁₀") thickness. Use a 6cm (2⅓") round cutter to stamp out about 24 circles, then using a small heart-shaped cutter, stamp out the centre of half of the biscuits. Place on a baking sheet and put into the fridge for 30 minutes.

Preheat the oven to 160°C fan (350°F).

Bake the biscuits for 12 minutes, or until pale golden. Leave on the baking sheets for 5 minutes then transfer to a wire rack to cool.

To assemble, spread about 1 teaspoon of jam or lemon curd on each of the whole biscuits then sandwich the biscuits together to create your jammy dodgers.

LAMBING-TONS

SERVES 16

INGREDIENTS

For the cake

125g (4½oz) butter

225g (8oz) sugar

½ teaspoon vanilla bean paste

3 eggs

225g (8oz) self-raising flour

125ml (½ cup) milk

For the icing

450g (1lb) icing sugar

25g (1oz) cocoa powder

125ml (½ cup) milk

1 tablespoon butter

300g (10½oz) desiccated coconut

When it comes to lambing time on the croft, my sister-in-law Seonag and brother Colin are up at 5 a.m. and regularly checking the sheep every couple of hours until sunset. It's hard work, but very rewarding. Seonag is a great baker and has given this classic Australian Lamington recipe a crofting makeover with the new name of Lambing-tons! This authentic recipe is one of the best things to come out of Oz since Kylie Minogue! If possible, make this cake a day ahead or at least give it lots of time to rest before slicing into squares.

METHOD

Preheat the oven to 160°C fan (350°F), grease and line a 20cm x 20cm (8" x 8") brownie pan.

Put the butter, sugar and vanilla in a mixing bowl and whisk until pale and fluffy. Beat in the eggs one at a time.

Sift in half the flour and combine. Stir in half the milk. Repeat with the remaining flour and milk. Spoon the batter into the prepared tin and spread out evenly. Bake for 25 minutes or until a skewer comes out cleanly.

Leave the cake to cool in the tin for 10 minutes, then turn out onto a wire rack (leave the baking paper in place). Cover and set aside overnight, or for as long as possible.

To make the icing, sift the icing sugar and cocoa powder into a large bowl. Warm the milk and butter in a small pan until the butter has melted. Add to the icing sugar and cocoa powder and stir until smooth.

Transfer the cake to a chopping board and peel away the baking paper. Trim away the side crusts and cut the remaining cake into 16 even squares.

Put the desiccated coconut in a shallow dish. Spear one piece of sponge onto a fork, hold it over a bowl and spoon the chocolate icing over until it is completely covered. Wait until the excess icing has dripped away then coat completely in the coconut. Once you have covered all the squares, place them on a wire rack and leave for 2 hours to set. Now you are ready to serve your Lambing-tons!

ISLAND FUDGE

MAKES 30 SQUARES

INGREDIENTS

397g (14oz) tin of
    condensed milk

150ml (½ cup +
    2 tablespoons) milk

450g (1lb) demerara sugar

115g (4oz) butter

2 tablespoons whisky

Okay, don't let the simple ingredients list fool you – to achieve the perfect whisky fudge is gonna take some muscle! I always have a back-up in the kitchen to take over the stirring and beating of the fudge until my arm stops tingling and I'm ready to get stuck in again! Making whisky fudge is an art that requires patience and precision – and a wee bit of power.

But fear not, as the reward is well worth the effort! This recipe creates a smooth, velvety fudge with a warmth from the whisky. If you can bear to part with these bite-sized treats, they make a lovely gift.

METHOD

Place all the ingredients, apart from the whisky, into a saucepan and melt over a low heat, stirring until the sugar dissolves.

Bring to a steady simmer for 15 minutes, stirring continuously. The mixture should reach up to a temperature of 113°C to 115°C (236°F to 239°F) on a thermometer.

Remove the fudge from the heat, leave to cool for 5 minutes then stir in the whisky. Beat the mixture for about 7 to 10 minutes until it becomes very thick and comes away from the sides of the pan.

With the back of a spoon press the fudge into a 20cm (8") square tin lined with baking parchment and leave to set for at least 3 hours before cutting into bite-sized squares.

WEE NUNS

MAKES 16

INGREDIENTS

170g (6oz) runny honey

85g (3oz) butter

110g (4oz) dark brown sugar

3 tablespoons vegetable oil

185ml (¾ cup + 1 teaspoon) water

200g (7oz) plain flour

80g (2¾oz) rye flour

1 teaspoon ground cinnamon

1 tablespoon mixed spice

2 teaspoons baking powder

1 teaspoon bicarbonate of soda

1 tablespoon dark rum

1 teaspoon vanilla bean paste

½ an orange, zested

1 egg yolk

5 tablespoons blackcurrant jam

Pinch of salt

Imagine yourself travelling through the Burgundy region of France during the Middle Ages. As you venture along the roads, you would have come across quite a sight – nuns stationed by the wayside, selling their homemade delights to passersby. Their jam-filled gingerbread cakes were particularly renowned, so much so that these treats became known as *Nonnettes*, named after the nuns themselves.

The tradition of Nonnettes continued to flourish over the centuries, and in 1796, a bakery by the name of Mulot & Petitjean opened its doors in Dijon. Their bakers embraced their legacy and proudly continued the tradition of these delightful cakes.

Nonnettes are petite gingerbread cakes crafted from a blend of fragrant honey, hearty rye flour and a harmonious medley of spices. But what truly sets them apart is their delectable filling – a generous dollop of luscious blackberry jam, adding a burst of fruity sweetness that beautifully complements the rich, spiced flavours.

METHOD

Preheat the oven to 170°C fan (375°F).

In a pan over a medium heat, add the honey, butter, sugar, oil and water, then stir until just melted. Remove and allow to cool slightly.

In a mixing bowl, add the flours, cinnamon and mixed spice, bicarbonate of soda, baking powder and salt. Stir to combine.

While it's still warm, pour the honey mixture into the flour and stir to combine. Stir in the rum, vanilla, orange zest and egg yolk.

Grease a mini cheesecake or mini muffin tin. Fill each space with batter between ½ to ⅔ full. Make an indentation in each one and place a teaspoon of jam in it.

Bake for 12 to 14 minutes until golden brown.

Allow your Wee Nuns to cool in the tin for 10 minutes, place on a wire rack to cool fully and then serve with an afternoon cuppa.

MARMALADE SHORTBREAD SANDWICH

MAKES 12

INGREDIENTS

250g (9oz) butter

125g (4½oz) golden caster sugar, plus extra for sprinkling

½ teaspoon vanilla bean paste

225g (8oz) plain flour

125g (4½oz) cornflour

50g (1¾oz) ground almonds

150g (5oz) marmalade

If Paddington Bear was from Portnaguran rather than Peru, this is the treat he'd be tucking into! The buttery and crumbly shortbread is filled with a generous layer of tangy, zesty marmalade. And, unlike Paddington, you don't need to keep this recipe under your hat – in fact, why not bake this for your auntie when she comes to visit? It'll become her new favourite treat!

METHOD

Preheat the oven to 160°C fan (350°F), and butter and line a 20cm (8") square cake tin with baking paper.

Put the butter, sugar and vanilla in a bowl, and beat with an electric whisk until light and creamy. Combine the flour, cornflour and ground almonds into the buttery mixture, then use your hands to bring everything together to a smooth dough. Divide the dough in half.

Roll out half of the dough and press into the base of the prepared tin; I like to use a whisky glass to get it as flat as possible. Spread over the marmalade.

Roll out the remaining dough on a piece of baking paper to a rough 20cm (8") square and carefully lift it on top of the marmalade. Lightly prick all over with a fork and bake for 35 to 40 minutes or until pale golden, then sprinkle with a little more sugar on top and leave in the tin to cool. Cut into 12 bars.

CUSTARD SLICE

A classic custard slice with silky smooth custard and crisp puff pastry is the ultimate teatime treat. This is pure nostalgia, and so much easier to make than you'd expect. Follow the recipe and the custard should set perfectly!

MAKES 8 SLICES

INGREDIENTS

2 x 320g (11¼oz) packs of ready-rolled puff pastry

For the custard

1 vanilla pod

500ml (2 cups) milk

100g (3½oz) sugar

4 eggs, yolks only

40g (1½oz) cornflour

40g (1½oz) butter

For the icing

200g (7oz) white chocolate

50g (1¾oz) dark chocolate

METHOD

Preheat your oven to 180°C fan (400°F) and line 2 baking trays with baking parchment.

Unroll your puff pastry and cut it into two 20cm (8") squares and place each square onto a lined baking tray. Cover each pastry square with some more parchment paper and then place a baking tray on top; this stops the pastry puffing up too much while baking.

Bake the pastry for 20 minutes until golden brown and place on a wire rack.

Now make the custard. Split the vanilla pod down the middle and scrape out the seeds. Pour the milk into a pan and add the pod and seeds. Bring the milk mixture to a simmer and remove from the heat.

Whisk the sugar, egg yolks and cornflour together in a large bowl.

Pour out a wee bit of the hot milk onto the egg mixture, whisking continuously. Whisk in the rest of the hot milk until well combined, then return to the pan.

Continually stir the mixture over a gentle heat, until it becomes thick. Remove from the heat and pass through a sieve. Add the butter and stir until thoroughly combined. Cover with clingfilm and leave to cool.

To create your slices

Line a 20cm x 20cm (8" x 8") square tin with baking parchment, making sure it folds over the edges of the tin.

Pop 1 square of pastry into the base of the tin, trimming it down slightly if it is too big. Pour your custard over the pastry and smooth it out.

Measure the second square of pastry to make sure it fits in the tin. Cut into 8 equally sized slices and place on top of the custard. Press lightly so it touches the custard layer and put it in the fridge to chill.

Now it's time to decorate. Break the white chocolate into pieces in a bowl. Melt the chocolate in the microwave for 20 second bursts. Repeat for the dark chocolate and pop it in a piping bag once melted.

Pour the melted white chocolate over the top of each of the pastry slices.

Now for the feathering. Pipe horizontal lines of dark chocolate spaced about 1 to 2cm (½ to ¾") apart over the top of the white chocolate. Grab a cocktail stick and pull vertically backwards and forwards to create your feathered chocolate effect.

Chill your custard slice in the fridge until the chocolate has set and you are ready to serve. Remove from the tin. Slice into 8 pieces and serve.

MILLIONAIRE KRISPY SQUARES

INGREDIENTS

For the base and caramel

125g (4½oz) soft dark brown sugar

125g (4½oz) butter

397g (14oz) tin of condensed milk

100g (3½oz) Rice Krispies or any rice cereal

For the topping

150g (5oz) milk chocolate

Though a slice of classic millionaire shortbread is near perfection on a plate, I have to say replacing the shortbread with a rice cereal base has made me fall in love with this three-layered treat all over again. It makes the recipe a bit more kid friendly, but find me an adult who wouldn't love this? Impossible!

METHOD

Line a 20cm x 20cm (8" x 8") brownie tin with baking parchment.

Heat the sugar and butter in a pan, gently stirring until melted. Add the condensed milk and bring to a boil, stirring continuously for a minute or so or until the caramel you have just created has thickened.

Put one-third of the caramel into a bowl and mix in the rice cereal. Gently press the mixture into the base of the tin and chill for about 15 minutes until set.

Pour the remaining caramel over the base. Cool, then chill for 30 minutes in the fridge until set.

Place half the chocolate into a bowl and microwave gently in 10 to 20 second bursts until melted, stirring occasionally. Then add the rest of the chocolate and stir together until melted. Now spread the chocolate over the caramel, then chill for 30 minutes until set.

Remove from the tin and cut into about 16 squares. Serve for adults and kids alike!

ABERNETHY CREAMS

MAKES A DOZEN

INGREDIENTS

For the biscuits

225g (8oz) plain flour

½ teaspoon baking powder

90g (3oz) butter, cubed

90g (3oz) sugar

¾ teaspoon caraway seeds

1 tablespoon milk

1 egg

For the buttercream

100g (3½oz) butter

200g (7oz) icing sugar

½ an orange, zested

Since their creation, Abernethy biscuits have stood the test of time, becoming a beloved classic in Scottish baking. Though many believe they originated in the Perthshire village of Abernethy, the truth is that these biscuits were originally crafted as a digestive aid by Dr John Abernethy during the eighteenth century.

I've turned them into a biscuit sandwich and added an orange-flavoured buttercream filling that complements the caraway seed-infused biscuits perfectly. Thanks, Doc!

METHOD

Preheat the oven to 170°C fan (375°F), then grease and line a baking sheet.

Into a bowl, sieve the flour and baking powder, then rub in the butter to make breadcrumbs. Mix in the sugar and caraway seeds before adding the milk and egg to form a dough.

Tip out onto a lightly floured surface and roll out to 2 to 3mm (1/10") thick and then use a cutter to cut into rounds.

Place slightly apart on a baking sheet and bake for 10 minutes until golden. Then, place on a wire rack to cool.

To make your buttercream, cream your butter and add the icing sugar, sifting it in 2 batches until smooth. Fold in the orange zest, then spread a buttercream layer on top of one biscuit and sandwich together with another.

CHOCOLATE CHIP OATCAKES

MAKES A DOZEN

INGREDIENTS

50ml (3 tablespoons +
  1 teaspoon) boiling water

50g (1¾oz) butter

50g (1¾oz) flour

50g (1¾oz) rolled oats

50g (1¾oz) pinhead oats

1 tablespoon sugar

40g (1½oz) dark chocolate
  chips

Pinch of salt

If you find yourself longing for something sweet yet wholesome, this recipe is just for you. At first glance, these oatcakes may seem virtuous with their hearty oats. However, don't be fooled – the chocolate adds a touch of sweetness that transforms them into a scrumptious treat that feels like an indulgence.

METHOD

Preheat the oven to 160°C fan (350°F), and line a baking tray with baking parchment.

Stir the boiling water into the butter until melted.

In a mixing bowl combine the flour, oats, sugar and salt, then pour the water and butter mixture over it and stir to combine. Mix to a dough, then cover the bowl with clingfilm and transfer it to the fridge to cool for 30 minutes. Once cooled, stir in the chocolate chips and knead until the chocolate is evenly distributed.

Roll the dough out to 2mm (1/10") thickness, then cut into rounds. Bake in the oven for 12 to 15 minutes until golden brown. Cool on a wire rack and serve.

HONEY ROCK CAKES

MAKES 8

INGREDIENTS

225g (8oz) flour

2 teaspoons baking powder

125g (4½oz) cold butter, cubed

35g (1¼oz) honey

2 tablespoons sugar, plus extra to sprinkle

75g (2½oz) sultanas

50g (1¾oz) glacé cherries, chopped

½ a lemon, zested

1 large egg, beaten

4 tablespoons milk

Rock cakes make a delightful addition to any tea-time spread, lunchbox treat, or simply enjoyed with a cuppa. Their rustic charm and nostalgic appeal will warm the hearts of any visitor to your kitchen. The honey not only adds a lovely aroma but also imparts a gentle sweetness that suits the Rock cakes perfectly.

METHOD

Preheat the oven to 160°C fan (350°F) and line 2 baking sheets.

Tip the flour and baking powder into a bowl. Rub in the butter with your fingertips to create a mix that looks like breadcrumbs.

Stir in the honey, sugar, sultanas, glacé cherries, lemon zest and egg, then stir through 3 tablespoons of the milk. Mix to form a thick, sticky batter, adding an extra tablespoon of milk if it's a little dry.

Spoon heaped tablespoons of your batter onto the lined baking sheets, leaving enough space for spreading.

Bake for 20 to 25 minutes until golden, sprinkle liberally with sugar and transfer to a wire rack to cool completely.

Cho eòlach 's a tha 'n ladar air a' phoit.

A MATCH MADE IN HEAVEN.

MY HEBRIDES
(PART II)

On the northwest of Scotland, you'll find a mosaic of islands, communities and seascapes known by names such as the Outer Hebrides, Western Isles, Suðreyar, Na h-Eileanan Siar, An t-Eilean Fada – our islands have been called many things throughout their history. One of my favourite names for the islands that stretch from Vatersay in the south to the island of Lewis in the north is Na h-Innse Gall, the Island of Strangers. This is how the Gaelic-speaking islanders referred to the settlement of the Norse Vikings in the Outer Hebrides in the tenth century.

Over the years many folk have arrived on the island as strangers, but have left with friends, husbands, wives and new families. Visitors will travel to see the Callanish Stones, our blackhouses and Museum nan Eilean in Stornoway to see the Lewis Chessmen. However, there exist countless other hidden treasures on our islands awaiting discovery.

But remember, don't tell anyone, it's our wee secret . . .

Julie Fowlis: Scottish Gaelic folk singer, multi-instrumentalist, radio and TV presenter, who has captivated audiences worldwide, breathing new life into the rich heritage of Scottish Gaelic music.
Only a short distance away from my home island of North Uist is the island of Berneray.

Growing up, the CalMac ferry took us there before the causeway was built in 1999. When I'm home, I take the trip over on my bike! I usually like to walk Tràigh Ear, East Beach, and swim in the clear green-blue sea. A hike to the highest point on the island, the trig point on Beinn Shlèibhe, is my next stop, before a stroll down to the stunning white beaches of Tràigh Iar, West Beach, on the far side of the island. From here you can see the hills of Harris, across to Àird a' Mhorain in North Uist and the beautiful islands of Pabaigh and Boraraigh. Rather than feeling like you are on the edge of the world, you feel like you are at the centre of the universe.

Douglas Stuart: the Booker Prize winning author of *Shuggie Bain* and *Young Mungo* is a Scottish-American author, screenwriter and fashion designer.
I feel the deepest connection to the loom sheds of the island's Harris Tweed weavers. Growing up in Glasgow, the men in my family never felt properly dressed unless they were wearing their Harris Tweed blazer. We didn't have much, but they took real pride in their appearance, and I can still feel the comforting scratch of my grandfather's tweed against my chin. As a boy, I was desperate for a tweed of my own. So, any time I visit Lewis, I make a pilgrimage to the mills, and

marvel at all the beautiful colours. I love the privilege of visiting a weaver at work, not only to see their craft in action – in a modern world that is increasingly automated, Harris Tweed remains one of the few cloths that are still made with care, and by hand – but also because an afternoon spent with a weaver usually yields some of the best stories around.

Calum Maclean: filmmaker, writer and outdoor swimmer, who is best known for his Instagram adventures in Scotland and on BBC Alba.
Here is a secret hidden beneath your feet. As you cross Abhainn a' Mhuil, the stream that marks the boundary of Lewis and Harris, you are greeted with roads signs: *'Fàilte do dh' Eilean Leòdhais'* and *'Fàilte do dh' Eilean na Hearadh'*. But hidden just out of sight is another welcome for the adventurous to find. Park in the nearby viewpoint on the Harris side, walk back over and then under the bridge to find the secret. Etched onto the road bridge is a poem of two halves; one side for Lewis, and one for Harris.

On the Lewis side: *Eilean Leòdhais, eilean bàigheil an fhraoich* – Lewis, the friendly heather isle.

And for Harris: *Eilean na Hearadh, eilean cùbhraidh nam beannaibh* – the scented hills of Harris.

Take a chance to listen to the stream that marks the border between Lewis and Harris and enjoy the views out to Eilean Shìophoirt.

Anne McAlpine: news anchor at BBC Scotland and presenter of the farming programme *Landward*.
Walking to the beach at Tràigh Shanndaidh in Eoropie, Ness, through the machair and dunes, is a treat in itself, with its glimpses of rare wildflowers, bumblebees and butterflies. It's not far from the Butt of Lewis – the most

northerly point of the island. The headland, which lies in the North Atlantic, is frequently battered by heavy swells and storms and is marked by the Butt of Lewis lighthouse. There's a walk you can do from the beach along the cliffs, which feels very exposed and rugged with the raging seas beneath you.

There's something very nostalgic about this beach for me, as it's within walking distance of my grandparents' house in Eoropie. Even with a 60mph wind thundering in from the wild Atlantic, you can't help but be blown away (pun intended) by its savage beauty.

Kate MacLeod: known as the Hebridean Mermaid, and host of *Miann na Maighdinn*, the award-winning BBC Alba show.
The stunning island of Taransay in Harris is home to one of my absolute favourite swim spots. Facing Luskentyre beach, it's a short distance by boat. Once ashore, walk up the pristine white beach to the machair, start your ascent up Beinn na h-Uidhe to the summit, then pause to take in one of the most spectacular views the Outer Hebrides has to offer.

After a few more minutes' walking, you'll come to Loch an Duin – a picturesque freshwater loch with an ancient, ruined fort situated in the middle.

Once in the water, you'll understand why it's one of my favourite spots – there is something truly magical about this place. The way the sunlight streams through the water makes you feel like you're in a dream – in another time and place altogether.

Duncan Chisholm: Scottish fiddle player, composer, solo musician and founding member of the folk-rock group Wolfstone.
On the west side of the Isle of Harris sits the island paradise of Scarp. From its peak of over 210 residents in the 1880s, the last

remaining islanders left there in 1971.

The island is reached by a short boat crossing across the Kyle of Scarp from Hushinish. There is a beach at the north end, surrounded by cliffs and caves at the strait between Scarp and Cearstaigh. The turquoise waters, the beach, the cliffs wrapped around the bay . . . all enveloped with a tranquillity seldom found anywhere else; it is utterly otherworldly.

Gary Innes: Scottish musician and composer, who is presenter of Radio Scotland's *Take the Floor* and a member of Scottish folk-rock band Mànran.
When thinking of a special location that means something to me, I get transported back to Lionacleit Beach on the Isle of Benbecula.

Just a stone's throw away from the island's airport, with its golden white sand that seems to never end and where the Atlantic Ocean laps at your toes. It was on this very beach that we celebrated our youngest daughter Margot's first birthday, while her big sister Gracie was in her happy place paddling and splashing in the turquoise-coloured water. It's definitely a destination you should never dream of visiting without your bucket and spade!

Katie MacLeod: award-winning writer from the Outer Hebrides, and founder of the travel blog Stories My Suitcase Could Tell.
My first stop when I'm at home in Lewis is Granny's Beach. It's not really called that, of course – locals call it the Tràigh – but because

it sits below the cliffs where my granny lived, as a wee girl I thought the beach was hers!

Although this small sweep of sand lies next to the bigger Bayble Beach, it's completely hidden out of sight. From the end of the beach road, follow the shoreline, which is fringed with sea pinks in the summer, and clamber over the rocks to the Tràigh. You'll probably be the only person there, and can admire the views of Bayble Island with just the oystercatchers for company.

DJ and Lindsay Cameron run Long Island Retreats, which hosts crofting experiences, pony tours and sheep shearing demonstrations for guests visiting South Uist.
On the rare days we take time off from the croft we venture over the hill to a wee bothy, which holds fond memories from nights spent there gathering sheep off the hill, with stories and a dram shared by the fire.

Accessed by boat or by a four-mile walk from Loch Skipport, Uisinis is one of South Uist's true hidden gems. The secluded bay at the bothy makes for a great picnic spot or for a wee swim to cool off after the walk in. Don't forget to follow the path round to the lighthouse to see red deer and eagles soaring above and to be rewarded with breathtaking views across to Skye and out to Canna and Rum.

But you ask, 'What about you, Coinneach? What's your secret spot on the islands?'

Well, that's easy. In my home village on the Isle of Lewis, there is the Cromore Walk. Waymarked by wooden posts, it takes you over the heather-clad hills hugging the island's southern coastline. The only folk you'll meet along the way are the sea eagles above you and the seals and otters swimming along the shoreline (and plenty of sheep, so keep dogs on a lead). Nearing the end of the walk, you'll arrive at Loch Cromore, where the remains of a drystone roundhouse tower, a *Dùn*, sits on a small island. If you have time and the tides are on your side, take a trip to the next village of Crobeag. From there, you can reach Eilean Chaluim Chille, St Columba's Island, the site where Columban monks first arrived in Lewis – they obviously had good taste!

Now, readers, who will be the first to visit all of our secret Hebridean locations? You'll deserve a cuppa and a cake after these adventures!

SHEARING CAKE

SERVES 8

INGREDIENTS

180g (6⅓oz) butter

150g (5oz) sugar

3 eggs

2 tablespoons plain yogurt or
   buttermilk

225g (8oz) self-raising flour

75g (2½oz) candied lemon
   peel or mixed peel

1 lemon, zested

2 teaspoons caraway seeds

Bella Cameron from South Uist has been a wonderful cook her whole life and still serves up delicious meals to guests visiting Grogarry Lodge on the island. With her son DJ busy on the croft with his cows, ponies and sheep, this traditional shearing cake is a perfect treat. Flavoured with lemon and caraway seeds . . . and baked to perfection!

METHOD

Preheat the oven to 160°C fan (350°F). Line and grease a 20cm (8") round cake tin.

Cream the butter and sugar together until light and fluffy. Beat in the eggs and yogurt or buttermilk. Then fold in the flour with a metal spoon until combined.

Gently stir in the candied peel, lemon zest and caraway seeds.

Spoon the mixture into the prepared cake tin, level the surface and bake in the preheated oven for an hour, until the cake is risen and a skewer comes out clean.

Remove from the oven and allow to cool for 10 to 15 minutes before turning out onto a wire rack. Leave to cool completely, then dust with icing sugar and serve.

WELSH CAKES

MAKES 8

INGREDIENTS

225g (8oz) self-raising flour

100g (3½oz) butter, cubed

50g (1¾oz) sugar, plus extra for sprinkling

50g (1¾oz) currants

1 egg

3 tablespoons milk

Pinch of salt

Welsh cakes, known as *Picau ar y Maen* in Welsh, meaning cakes on the stone, are a beloved traditional treat that has delighted generations in the heart of Cymru.

These griddle cakes are the epitome of buttery goodness and sweetness, thanks to the addition of currants and a generous dusting of sugar. Don't worry if you don't have a griddle – a trusty cast-iron pan will work just as well.

METHOD

Mix the flour and salt together in a large bowl and rub in the butter until the mixture resembles breadcrumbs. Add the sugar and currants and stir well.

Beat the egg and combine with the milk and mix in until you have a stiff dough.

Roll the dough out on a lightly floured board until 5mm (⅕") thick and stamp out rounds with a cookie cutter.

Heat the griddle over a medium heat until hot and grease with a little butter. Cook the cakes for about 3 to 4 minutes each side, until they are golden brown and have risen slightly.

Serve immediately, sprinkled with a little extra sugar.

Cha 'n fhaodar a' bhò a reic 's a bainne òl.

YOU CAN'T HAVE YOUR CAKE AND EAT IT.

CORNISH SAFFRON BUNS

MAKES 8 TO 10

INGREDIENTS

For the buns

0.4g saffron strands

300ml (1¼ cup) milk

90g (3oz) clotted cream

50g (1¾oz) butter

550g (1lb 4oz) strong white
bread flour

1¼ teaspoons sea salt

50g (1¾oz) golden caster
sugar

7g (¼oz) sachet fast-acting
dried yeast

70g (2½oz) raisins

30g (1oz) mixed peel

For the glaze

50g (1¾oz) golden caster
sugar

2 tablespoons water

Dydh da, ow hanow yw, Coinneach!

Kernewek, the Cornish language, is part of the Celtic family, though much
more related to Welsh and Breton than to Irish and Gaelic. These are a
Cornish classic: golden fruited buns infused with saffron which are best
when still warm, sliced in half and smothered in butter. These tasty treats are
dedicated to the Greening family down in Camborne.

METHOD

Crush the saffron strands between your fingertips in a small bowl.

Heat the milk in a pan until simmering. Remove from the heat then add the
saffron. Stir in the clotted cream and butter until fully melted. Set aside to
infuse for 15 to 20 minutes until golden.

Combine the flour, salt, sugar and yeast in the bowl. Make a well in the
centre and add the milk. Stir to combine to create a dough, then knead on
a lightly floured surface for about 5 minutes.

Add the raisins and mixed peel and continue to knead for a further
5 minutes.

Cover the bowl with a clean tea towel and leave to rise in a warm place
for about an hour, or until doubled in size.

When risen, turn the dough out onto a floured board and knock it back and
knead for a further couple of minutes.

Divide the dough into 8 to 10 even pieces and roll each piece into a ball.
Place on a baking sheet, cover with your clean tea towel and leave to rise
again for about 30 minutes.

Preheat the oven to 180°C fan (400°F), then bake the buns for 20 minutes
until golden.

For the glaze

Put the golden caster sugar and water in a saucepan. Gently heat until
dissolved then boil for a minute before brushing the glaze over the warm
buns. Transfer to a wire rack and leave to cool.

Slice in half and enjoy the buns fresh or toasted, spread with clotted cream
or butter.

FAR BRETON

SERVES 6

INGREDIENTS

175g (6¼oz) prunes

50ml (3 tablespoons + 1 teaspoon) dark rum

130g (4½oz) sugar

4 eggs

110g (4oz) plain flour

750ml (3 cups) milk

50g (1¾oz) butter

Pinch of salt

Far Breton, or *far aux pruneaux*, is a delicious prune-infused custard pudding from Brittany, where it is served as a breakfast dish or a dessert . . . or both; I always love a breakfast pudding! A Far Breton has similarities to a clafoutis, both being egg-based custards with the addition of flour.

As the custard bakes to perfection, it envelops the succulent rum-soaked prunes. Prunes appear a lot in Breton recipes; it's said that fishermen from Brittany used to trade their catch for Agen prunes.

METHOD

Add your prunes to a bowl, cover in rum and soak for a few hours, or ideally overnight.

Place a baking tray in the oven and preheat to 220°C fan (465°F). Meanwhile, mix the sugar and eggs together and add the flour gradually, then a pinch of salt. Whisk in the cold milk to make a thin batter and set to one side.

Grease a 1½ litre (1½ quarts) ovenproof dish with butter, scatter in the prunes and put the dish on the heated baking tray into the oven for 10 minutes, or until the butter browns. Pour in the batter and return it to the oven for 10 minutes, then reduce the heat to 180°C fan (400°F) and bake for another 40 minutes, until dark golden and risen. If it gets too dark, cover with foil for the last 10 minutes.

Serve your Far Breton warm as a dessert, or cooled and sliced as a cake. *Mes compliments au chef!*

APPLE GÂTEAU BRETON

SERVES 4 TO 6

INGREDIENTS

350g (12½oz) plain flour

250g (9oz) butter, cubed

250g (9oz) golden caster sugar

2 teaspoons vanilla bean paste

5 egg yolks, plus 1 whole egg

1 tablespoon dark rum

1 cooking apple

First known as a Lorient Cake, this rich, buttery cake was entered into a pastry competition at the Paris Universal Exhibition by Louis Crucer – a competition which it deservedly won. In a twist to its story, French domestic servant Hélène Jégado is believed to have killed as many as 36 people by serving them her baked Gâteau Breton poisoned with arsenic! Rather than Hélène's choice of filling, you can choose to make your prize-winning cake plain, with apples, prunes or even a caramel.

METHOD

Grease and line a 20cm (8") loose-bottomed cake tin.

With your fingertips, rub the flour, butter and sugar together until the mixture looks like fine breadcrumbs.

Whisk together the vanilla, egg yolks and rum with a fork and mix into the dry ingredients to form a dough. Divide the mixture into 2 equal portions and chill in the fridge for at least an hour.

Preheat the oven to 160°C fan (350°F).

Press a portion of the dough into the prepared cake tin. Peel and slice your apple, and arrange the slices on top, pressing down gently and leaving a small border around the edge. Roll out the remaining piece of dough and place on top of the apples.

Brush with the beaten whole egg, then use a fork to lightly trace a criss-cross pattern on top of the dough. Bake for 40 minutes until golden.

BRETON MADELEINES

MAKES 16

INGREDIENTS

100g (3½oz) Breton butter

2 large eggs

100g (3½oz) golden caster
sugar

1 tablespoon honey

100g (3½oz) self-raising
flour

Pinch of sea salt

Icing sugar, to serve

With their signature scalloped shell shape and golden exterior, the brown butter in these madeleines, made with Breton butter, infuses the cakes with a rich, nutty flavour that complements their delicate sponge texture to perfection. Dust with icing sugar and serve warm from the oven.

METHOD

Melt the butter in a small saucepan until sizzling. Now, watch carefully: the butter will foam and, when the foam subsides, it will turn from yellow to a hazelnut brown – this is when you need to catch it. Remove from the heat and leave to cool.

Preheat the oven to 190°C fan (410°F) and butter a 12-hole madeleine tin.

Beat the eggs, sugar and honey together, then add the flour and salt, and finally mix in the butter.

Spoon the mixture into the madeleine holes and bake for 8 to 10 minutes or until puffed up and golden. Turn out onto a wire rack to cool while you cook a second batch. Dust the just-warm madeleines with icing sugar and serve.

IRISH APPLE TART

SERVES 6

INGREDIENTS

For the pastry

250g (9oz) flour

125g (4½oz) cold butter, cubed

25g (1oz) sugar

5 to 6 tablespoons cold water

For the filling

6 Pink Lady apples, peeled, cored and thinly sliced (roughly weighing 1kg; 2.2lb)

50g (1¾oz) sugar

1 tablespoon milk

1 egg, beaten

This is a beloved Irish classic dessert. There's something magical about its simplicity; it possesses a sense of comfort with every bite. Whether it's thanks to the perfect balance of sweetness and tartness or the tender apples encased in a buttery, golden crust, this is the only apple tart recipe I use.

METHOD

Preheat the oven to 140°C fan (325°F) and grease a 23cm (9") ovenproof plate.

Sift the flour into a large bowl and chill in the fridge, with the butter, for 30 minutes. Take out the flour and the butter from the fridge, then use your fingertips to rub the flour, butter and sugar together until the mixture looks like fine breadcrumbs. Add the tablespoons of cold water and, using a knife, bring the dough together.

Divide the pastry dough in half. Roll out half the pastry to the size of your ovenproof plate and lay it across. Take your apple slices, sprinkle on the sugar and arrange over the pastry, leaving a 2cm (¾") gap around the outside edge.

Brush the edge of the pastry with a little milk. Roll out the second piece of pastry into a circle slightly larger than the dish and use it to cover the apples. Press the edges together to seal, then use a sharp knife to cut away any excess.

Crimp the edges of the tart with a round-bladed knife, roll out the pastry scraps and cut them into leaf shapes. Brush the shapes with milk and place on top of the pie.

Cut 4 slits into the pastry near the centre to release the steam. Brush the pastry with the beaten egg wash to create a golden crust. Bake in the preheated oven for 35 to 40 minutes or until the pastry is golden brown and the apples are cooked. Serve with cream, custard or ice cream.

STOUT CHOCOLATE BROWNIES

MAKES A DOZEN

INGREDIENTS

330ml (1½ cup) Guinness

350g (12½oz) golden caster sugar

50ml (3 tablespoons + 1 teaspoon) double cream

250g (9 oz) butter

250g (9oz) dark chocolate, chopped

3 eggs

1 teaspoon vanilla bean paste

75g (2½oz) plain flour

50g (1¾oz) cocoa powder

Pinch of sea salt

The bittersweet notes of dark chocolate harmonise perfectly with the robust undertones of the hearty stout, resulting in a brownie that is rich, moist and deeply flavoursome. These Guinness brownies do not taste like beer! With its roast coffee and caramelised flavours, the Guinness not only intensifies chocolate, but adds a malty background. Serve with vanilla ice cream.

METHOD

Into a pan, add the Guinness and allow it to reduce by half over a medium/high heat, then pour half into a jug and leave the rest to cool in the pan.

Add 50g (1¾oz) of the sugar into a frying pan on a high heat, cook until caramelised, swirling the pan occasionally. Pour in the cream and swirl the pan to dissolve the sugar. Add in 25g (¾oz) of the butter and the Guinness from the jug. Stir and simmer for 2 to 3 minutes until you have a smooth, dark caramel. Leave aside to cool.

Meanwhile, preheat the oven to 160°C fan (350°F). Grease and line the base of a 20cm x 20cm (8" x 8") brownie tin.

Return the pan of Guinness to a low heat, stir in the remaining 225g (8oz) of butter and 200g (7oz) of the dark chocolate until melted. Remove from the heat, whisk in 300g (10½oz) of sugar, the eggs and vanilla bean paste. Whisk in the flour, cocoa and salt until smooth. Stir in the remaining 50g (1¾oz) of chocolate.

Pour half the mixture into the tin and, using a knife, swirl through half the caramel. Repeat with the remaining brownie batter and caramel. Bake for 30 minutes or until the edges are set but the middle is still a bit jiggly. Leave to cool, then cut into 12 squares to serve.

ISLAND LIFE

My grandfather Murdo and my granny Margaret were born just a few months apart in 1896, only a few houses away from each other in the village of Cromore on the Isle of Lewis. They both ventured off the island to find work: Murdo to the Merchant Navy and Margaret to a grand house in Edinburgh to work as a chambermaid. But then they settled back in Cromore, where they made their home in a blackhouse on the family croft after they married in Glasgow in the early 1920s.

Their home looked over Loch Cromore and was built with double drystone walls packed with earth, roofed with a thatch of turf and straw. The floor was packed earth with a central hearth for the fire. They were not the only ones living in the blackhouse; the family lived at one end and the animals lived at the other, providing extra warmth during the winter storms.

At the turn of the twentieth century, over two hundred people lived in the village and, unlike today, where most villagers need to travel to Stornoway to do their shopping, you could buy most things you needed in the village.

The bakery was named Bùth Iain Sheonaidh and was the centre of life in the village with all the *bodachs* debating life in and around the shop. Bùth Fhionnlaigh sold everything from chickens to paraffin, which they shipped over by boat from Stornoway every week.

But the most notable shop was Bùth Mhurchaidh Iain Chalum owned by another local named Murdo. He was a real character with a long beard down to his knees and a crooked walking stick. All the same, he must have been quite a ladies' man, as he was married four times! He was most famous for his homebrew that he named *Dealanaich MhicConnachie*, which was made in his still and served at all the cèilidhs in the village.

The shop came to a sticky end one night when a fierce gale blew the roof off all the way across the village. Many items that had hung from the rafters, including bags of fruit, were strewn across the fields and children were busy collecting the spoils throughout the village for days ahead! After he lost his shop, he replaced it with a horse and cart – at the time, the only one in the village – which he used to hire out for the locals to bring home their peats and transport their lambs.

As the rest of the island developed, Cromore seemed to be left isolated on the southeast coast. On 6 January 1900, a letter appeared in the *Highland News* from a reader in Cromore. In desperation, he pleaded for there to be a road built that would allow the locals to venture safely from the village.

For a number of years, we have been endeavouring to have a road constructed through the wild and trackless moors which lie south of Loch Erisort. We have repeatedly consulted our Parish and County Councillors, but have hitherto met with no success.

All our traffic with Stornoway is carried on by means of small open boats, the only kind at our disposal. As rough seas – sometimes in summer, but most frequently in winter – intercept our communication with the town, often for several days at a time, we are storm-stayed at Stornoway sometimes for upwards of six days at a time, when we might otherwise be usefully employed at home.

Even on our way home we are caught in sudden storms, when, after battling with the elements for hours, we are compelled to yield to them and make for the most sheltered cove available, where we must stay, completely sea-soaked, protected only by the inhospitable cliffs, until the storm subsides and finally arrive home with goods damaged and in many instances rendered perfectly useless.

Surely we are not condemned to live much longer under such trying circumstances when a few miles of road would cause them all to vanish, for if we had a road from Cromore to Gravir and on to Lemreway with short branches to Marvig and Calbost, all these difficulties, which cannot be realised by any except those who have experienced them, could be avoided. We hope that our councillors will kindly take up our cause once more.

It took another two decades before the road was finally complete, and one member of the crew was my grandfather, Murdo MacLeod, or as he was known in Gaelic, Murchadh an Time.

The lives of Murdo and Margaret changed forever in 1926 when they applied for a loan from the Department of Agriculture and Fisheries to build their own modern home. They received £250 and fifty years to pay it back in two instalments a year of £3 ⅝ pence.

Until the Crofters Act in 1886, no crofter built a permanent dwelling house for fear of being evicted at short notice, at the whim of the landlord or his tyrannical factor. But from 1910, houses began to be built in the village and many are still standing today.

The house was finished in 1927, just in time for their daughter Bellag (a younger sister for Angus) to be born in 1928. My Aunt Bellag remembers being called the first visitor to the new house!

Young Bellag's life in Cromore revolved around the rhythms of nature and the land. The family tended to a flock of sheep and three cows, and she dutifully planted potatoes, cut hay and milked the cows every morning and night with her mother.

The school had been built in the village in the late 1870s and, when Bellag attended along with her best friend Kate from the next croft, they were first tasked with learning English, a whole new language after spending the first five years of their lives only speaking Gaelic. She would walk to school, and during the summer, she would come home for lunch. Food was scarce during those times, and a plate of potato soup or a bowl of porridge was often served as the midday meal. Over forty children were in the school at the time and every Monday morning their teacher, Mrs MacKenzie, would travel by boat over from her home in Crossbost to return on Friday.

Christmas was a humble affair in Cromore, as money was scarce, and presents were a luxury they could not afford. However, the arrival of the New Year was cause for celebration. The villagers would come together by Bùth Iain Sheonaidh where a beer keg would be placed alongside some bottles

of *Dealanaich MhicConnachie* homebrew from Bùth Mhurchaidh Iain Chalum, their shoes worn out from dancing all night to the tunes of the melodeon.

Just two years before Bellag married Murdo in 1956, electricity was brought to the village and, when they returned from their wedding ceremony in Inverness, they hosted a celebration in both Cromore and Marvig, the village where Murdo was born and where they would make their home. A special dinner was prepared, and to commemorate the occasion, the local bard, Murdani Mast, composed a song in their honour.

The story of Bellag's upbringing in the village of Cromore is one that reflects a close-knit community, and the challenges and resilience of a simple life. It is a tale of hard work, shared laughter, and the strength that comes from family and cherished traditions, forever tied to the land and the sea that shaped her.

A SPOONFUL OF HYGGE

5

BANANA DUFF

SERVES 8 TO 10

INGREDIENTS

225g (8oz) plain flour

1 teaspoon bicarbonate of soda

1 teaspoon mixed spice

1 teaspoon cinnamon

175g (6¼oz) sugar

100g (3½oz) suet, vegetarian or beef, as you prefer

100g (3½oz) sultanas

75g (2½oz) currants

75g (2½oz) raisins

150g (5oz) banana, peeled

75ml (⅓ cup) buttermilk

1 egg, beaten

1 heaped tablespoon black treacle

Pinch of salt

Did you really expect a Hebridean Baker cookbook without another Duff recipe? You know I love a traditional Clootie Dumpling, especially my Aunt Bellag's recipe from my first cookbook. But I think I might have given this classic boiled fruit cake the ultimate upgrade here: I've combined the comforting flavours of banana loaf with the timeless appeal of a Duff.

Banana Duff, or B'uff for short! I just wonder what my Aunt Bellag is going to say.

METHOD

Everything goes in one bowl. Sieve your flour and add your bicarbonate of soda, mixed spice, cinnamon and salt into a bowl and combine.

Add your sugar, suet and dried fruits to the bowl and stir together.

Mash your bananas and add to the bowl along with your buttermilk, beaten egg and black treacle. Combine together.

Place a piece of muslin cloth or a cotton dishtowel (the cloot) in boiling water, and once cool enough to touch, wring the cloth out. Place the cloth on your work surface and sprinkle liberally with flour.

Place the mixture into the centre of the cloot. Gather up the edges of the cloth and, with a length of string, tie up (but not too tightly), leaving some room for the dumpling to expand.

In a large pan of boiling water (deep enough to cover the dumpling), place a saucer upside down. Place the dumpling onto the saucer, cover with a lid and simmer for 3 hours. Don't let the water evaporate; you may need to top it up.

Take out of the pan and carefully remove the cloot from the dumpling, trying not to take off any of the 'skin'. In a warm kitchen, let it rest for 30 minutes before slicing.

LEMON CURD TIRAMISU

SERVES 6

INGREDIENTS

For the syrup

100g (3½oz) sugar

2 lemons, zested and juiced

50ml (3 tablespoons + 1 teaspoon) water

50ml (3 tablespoons + 1 teaspoon) limoncello

For the mascarpone cream

500g (1lb 2oz) mascarpone

600ml (2½ cups) double cream

3 tablespoons icing sugar

50g (1¾oz) lemon curd

1 lemon, zested

1 tablespoon fresh lemon juice

50ml (3 tablespoons + 1 teaspoon) limoncello

200g (7oz) savoiardi sponge fingers

To serve

2 tablespoons lemon curd

Leftover syrup

Although our Hebridean summers may be short, when the sun does appear over the islands, there is nowhere more beautiful in the world. This lemon curd tiramisu is definitely a celebration dessert. You can let the citrusy flavours from the lemons, the curd and limoncello do the hard work; all you need to do is make perfect layers of the savoiardi 'ladyfingers' sponges and the lightly whipped mascarpone cream. For those seeking the secret to homemade lemon curd, turn to the pages of *My Scottish Island Kitchen* cookbook.

METHOD

In a pan, heat the sugar, zest and juice of the lemons with the water. Cook over a low heat until the sugar is melted, then bring up to a boil and reduce for 2 to 3 minutes. Leave to one side to cool for 5 minutes, then stir in the limoncello.

In a bowl, whisk the mascarpone until smooth. Then lightly beat in the cream, icing sugar, lemon curd, lemon zest, lemon juice and limoncello.

One by one, lightly soak half of the sponge fingers in the syrup (remember to save a little for serving), then lay them across a 20cm x 30cm (8" x 12") ceramic dish or into individual dishes. Spoon over half of the limoncello cream. Repeat with the remaining sponge fingers and cream. Leave to set in the fridge for at least 3 hours.

When ready to serve, drizzle over the lemon curd and some of the leftover limoncello syrup.

ATHOLL BROSE CHEESECAKE

SERVES 4 TO 6

INGREDIENTS

For the Atholl Brose

250ml (1 cup) whisky

70g (2½oz) oats

3 teaspoons honey

40ml (2 tablespoons +
2 teaspoons) double
cream

For the cheesecake

100g (3½oz) butter

250g (9oz) digestive biscuits,
crushed

600g (1lb 5oz) cream
cheese

35ml (2 tablespoons +
1 teaspoon) Atholl Brose

100g (3½oz) icing sugar

300ml (1¼ cup) double
cream

100g (3½oz) dark
chocolate, grated

Imagine Atholl Brose as a fifteenth-century Scottish drink reminiscent of a Bailey's Irish Cream! Now you'll realise why this is the perfect flavouring for this creamy, no-bake cheesecake. Remember, you'll need to start your prep at least a day before you'd like to make the cheesecake. I have made enough here for you to share a dram of the Brose while you devour this delicious dessert. *Slàinte!*

METHOD

To make the Atholl Brose

To make the Brose, pour the whisky over the oats in a bowl and rest under a clean dishtowel for 24 hours.

The next day, use a muslin (or cotton dishtowel) to squeeze out the whisky into a fresh bowl. Be sure to get every last drop! You can discard the oats.

Warm up your honey for 10 seconds in the microwave, or over a low heat in a small pan, and whisk into the Brose mix.

Add your cream and whisk again. Now let it rest in the fridge for at least 4 hours.

To make the cheesecake

First, melt the butter in a pan, remove from the heat and add the crushed digestive biscuits. Mix well until the biscuits have absorbed all the butter.

Press into the bottom of a lined 18cm (7") springform tin. Place in the fridge and allow to set for an hour.

Meanwhile, prepare the filling. Lightly whip the cream cheese then beat in the Atholl Brose and icing sugar. Whip the cream and fold in along with the grated chocolate. When smooth, spoon evenly onto the biscuit base.

Refrigerate and allow to set for a further 2 hours, then serve with a dram of Atholl Brose.

CHERRY BAKEWELL STEAMED PUDDING

SERVES 4

INGREDIENTS

For the pudding

115g (4oz) butter

115g (4oz) sugar

2 eggs

50g (1¾oz) marzipan, grated

50g (1¾oz) glacé cherries, chopped

1 teaspoon almond extract

175g (6¼oz) plain flour

1 teaspoon baking powder

For the sauce

90ml (¼ cup + 2 tablespoons) cherry jam

150ml (½ cup + 2 tablespoons) water

1 tablespoon arrowroot powder

A trickle of cherry jam tops this classic steamed pudding with the flavours of a Bakewell tart. This is a dish so comforting and warming, you'll need to serve it to your guests while they're on the sofa in front of the fire. Be sure to have a jug of custard ready for anyone who needs an extra treat!

For the steaming, I used a pudding basin with a lid. If yours doesn't have one, lay a piece of baking parchment on top of a sheet of foil, making a large pleat in the middle, to allow the pudding to rise. Cover the basin foil side up, crimp around the sides and secure tightly with string.

METHOD

Lightly grease a 900ml (3¾ cups) pudding basin.

In a bowl, cream together the butter and sugar until pale and light, then whisk in the eggs. Grate your marzipan, chop your cherries and stir these in along with the almond extract.

Sift the flour and baking powder, then fold into the batter. Spoon your mix into the prepared basin, smooth the top and put the lid on.

In a large saucepan filled halfway with boiling water, place a saucer upside down and put the pudding basin on top. Allow that to simmer with the lid on for 2 hours. Keep an eye on the pan and top up the water if necessary.

To make the sauce, first sieve the jam into a small saucepan along with 120ml (½ cup) of water. Blend the arrowroot powder with 30ml (2 tablespoons) of cold water and stir into the jam mixture. Stirring all the time, heat the sauce gently until it boils and begins to thicken.

To serve, carefully invert the pudding onto a serving plate. Serve warm with the hot cherry jam sauce.

BLACK TREACLE & GINGERNUT ICE CREAM

MAKES 12 SERVINGS

INGREDIENTS

4 egg yolks

½ tablespoon golden caster sugar

3 tablespoons black treacle

200ml (¾ cup + 1 tablespoon) milk

250ml (1 cup) double cream

3 gingernut biscuits, chopped

Since its launch in 1950, Lyle's Black Treacle has earned a special place in every Scottish kitchen. Its unique, robust flavour with a subtle touch of bitterness has made it a beloved ingredient in scones, Christmas cakes and gingerbread. Now, imagine infusing this distinctive treasure into a homemade ice cream. The result is pure magic. To enhance, I've incorporated gingernuts, allowing them to soften while imparting a delightful burst of spice in every spoonful.

METHOD

Whisk the egg yolks, sugar and treacle in a large bowl until creamy.

In a pan over a low heat, add the milk and 100ml (⅓ cup + 2 tablespoons) of cream until it begins to simmer. Then remove from the heat and gradually whisk into the treacle mixture and allow to cool.

Once the mixture is completely cold, whip the extra 150ml (½ cup + 2 tablespoons) cream and whisk it all together until completely combined.

Place in a box suitable for a freezer and freeze for 90 minutes.

Take the box out of the freezer and stir the frozen and soft ice cream together, then add the chopped pieces of gingernut biscuits and fold into the ice cream. Place the box back into the freezer and repeat the stirring 2 more times.

Bring your tub of ice cream out of the freezer about 15 minutes before you plan to serve.

ANGUS' KIRSCH CAKE

SERVES 8

INGREDIENTS

For the cake

6 eggs

1 teaspoon vanilla bean paste

250g (9oz) golden caster sugar

50g (1¾oz) cocoa powder

100g (3½oz) plain flour

150g (5oz) butter, melted and cooled

For the syrup

200ml (¾ cup + 1 tablespoon) water

175g (6¼oz) golden caster sugar

2 tablespoons kirsch

For the kirsch cream

750ml (3 cups) whipping cream

75g (2½oz) golden caster sugar

2 teaspoons vanilla bean paste

3 tablespoons kirsch

For the toppings

3 tablespoons cherry jam

410g (14½oz) tin of black cherries (I use Princes Fillings & Toppings)

150g (5oz) dark chocolate, grated

Handful of fresh cherries

When your father is a master whisky distiller, then you'll know a good dram. But Angus can not only choose the right *uisge beatha* to serve you, he is also one of the best bakers on Islay. His signature dessert is a layered cherry and chocolate cake with a boozy whipped cream, which really is a showstopper dessert to bring to the table. As the island doctor, I think he should be prescribing a slice of his kirsch cake every day!

METHOD

Preheat the oven to 160°C fan (350°F). Grease and line three 22cm (8½") sandwich cake tins.

In a bowl, whisk the eggs, vanilla and sugar together using an electric hand whisk until thick – it will take about 10 minutes. Fold in the sifted cocoa powder and flour together, then stir in the cooled, melted butter.

Divide the cake mixture between the tins and bake for 20 minutes until a skewer comes out clean. Rest in the tins for 5 minutes and turn out onto wire racks to cool.

To make the syrup, put the water and the sugar in a pan, then bring to the boil for 5 minutes. Leave to cool and stir in the kirsch. To make the kirsch cream, whip the cream and sugar to firm peaks, then fold in the vanilla and kirsch.

To assemble your cake

Place the first sponge on the serving plate and brush over the syrup, then spread over a layer of cherry jam. Top with the next sponge, brush with the syrup, spread a layer of the kirsch cream, and top with the tinned cherries.

Spread a little more cream over the cherries, top with the final sponge and brush with syrup.

Place about a quarter of the remaining cream into a piping bag, then use the rest of the cream to cover the top and sides of the cake. Pipe the cream in swirls on the top of the cake.

Grate the chocolate and press onto the sides of the cake with your hands. Finally, place the fresh cherries on top of the cake and serve. Just what the doctor ordered!

DRUNKEN CRUMBLE

SERVES 6

INGREDIENTS

For the filling

4 cooking apples, like
  Bramley
  (about 700g/1lb 9oz)

25g (¾oz) sugar

½ teaspoon ground
  cinnamon

Pinch of freshly ground
  nutmeg

75ml (⅓ cup) spiced rum

½ a lemon, zested and
  juiced

3 eating apples, like
  Braeburn
  (about 400g/14oz)

For the crumble topping

125g (4½oz) cold butter,
  diced

200g (7oz) plain flour

125g (4½oz) light
  muscovado sugar

30g (1oz) rolled oats

30g (1oz) flaked almonds

This boozy pud will put some colour in your cheeks! The mix of cooking and eating apples creates a lovely combination of textures along with the crunch from the oaty almond topping. As the apples gently bake, their natural sweetness infuses with the warm spices and rum to make a delicious autumnal dessert.

METHOD

Preheat the oven to 170°C fan (375° F) and butter a 20cm x 20cm (8" x 8") baking dish.

Peel and roughly chop the cooking apples into large chunks. Place into a saucepan, and add the sugar, cinnamon, nutmeg, rum, lemon zest and juice. Bring to a simmer, cover and cook for 5 minutes or until the apples have started to soften. Remove from the heat.

Peel and chop the eating apples into similar sized chunks, add together, then tip into the baking dish. Allow the fruit to cool down before adding the crumble topping.

To make the crumble topping, rub the butter into the flour with your fingertips until the mixture looks like breadcrumbs. Stir in the sugar, oats and almonds, then scatter the topping over the cooled fruit.

Bake in the oven for 40 minutes until the topping is golden and crisp, and the juices are starting to bubble up around the edges. Allow to rest for 5 minutes, then serve with your choice of custard, ice cream or pouring cream.

*Am fear a bhios a' riarachadh na maraig' bidh
an ceann reamhar aige fhèin.*

WHOEVER SLICES THE PUDDING TAKES THE BIGGEST SHARE.

DUNDEE MARMALADE SOUFFLÉ

SERVES 6

INGREDIENTS

For the soufflé

175g (6¼oz) marmalade, plus an extra teaspoon for each ramekin

5 egg whites

Pinch of salt

To serve

20g (¾oz) icing sugar

When you need a quick homemade dessert with a Scottish flavour, this can be whipped up and on the table in 20 minutes. Make sure the eggs are at room temperature before whisking and be gentle when you fold them into the marmalade. You can make these soufflés as elegant or as topsy-turvy as you like. Rest assured, they will hold their shape and won't collapse before making their grand appearance at the table.

METHOD

Preheat the oven to 170°C fan (375°F).

Add the marmalade into a large bowl and loosen it with a fork.

Put the egg whites in a metal bowl, add a pinch of salt and whisk until they reach stiff peaks. Fold a spoonful of the egg whites into the marmalade, then fold in the rest a spoonful at a time.

Place a teaspoon of marmalade into each ramekin, then divide the mixture between the ramekins, piling it up as high as possible.

Place the ramekins on a baking tray in the centre of the oven and cook for 10 minutes until your soufflé tops are browned. Dust with icing sugar and serve immediately.

NOVA SCOTIA BLUEBERRY GRUNT

SERVES 6

INGREDIENTS

For the filling

200ml (¾ cup +
    1 tablespoon) water

100g (3½oz) sugar

1 teaspoon lemon juice

½ teaspoon cinnamon

700g (1lb 9oz) blueberries

For the dumplings

240g (8½oz) plain flour

2 teaspoons baking powder

½ teaspoon bicarbonate of
    soda

60g (2oz) cold butter, cubed

225ml (¾ cup +
    3 tablespoons) buttermilk

Pinch of salt

On my first trip to Nova Scotia on Canada's beautiful east coast, I was served a blueberry grunt. Naturally, my first question was, 'What's with the funny name?' Well, seemingly while the dumplings are cooking over the fruit filling, if you put your ear to the skillet, you will hear the blueberries begin to grunt! It's very similar to a cobbler, but a grunt is traditionally cooked on the stove top and covered with a lid instead of baked in the oven.

And, even if you don't hear the grunt, you will still have a delicious pudding!

METHOD

To make the filling, add the water, sugar, lemon juice and cinnamon into an ovenproof skillet or Dutch oven. Once simmering, stir in the blueberries and allow them to cook gently for 15 to 20 minutes.

To make the dumplings, sieve the flour, baking powder, bicarbonate of soda and salt into a large bowl.

Rub the butter into the flour with your fingertips until the mixture looks like breadcrumbs. Stir in the buttermilk to make a dough.

Dollop heaped tablespoons of the dough over the blueberry mixture. Cover and cook for 15 minutes over a low heat until the biscuits are cooked through. Totally optional, but to add a little colour to the dumplings, place the skillet under the grill for 3 to 4 minutes until the dumplings get crispy edges.

Serve with ice cream or clotted cream.

PEAR EVE'S PUDDING & GINGERBREAD CUSTARD

SERVES 4

INGREDIENTS

For the filling

500g (1lb 2oz) pears

20g (¾oz) butter

1 tablespoon lemon juice

2 tablespoons sugar

For the topping

75g (2½oz) butter

100g (3½oz) sugar

100g (3½oz) self-raising flour

2 eggs, lightly beaten

1 tablespoon boiling water

For the custard

4 egg yolks

1 tablespoon sugar

1 heaped teaspoon cornflour

300ml (1¼ cup) milk

1 vanilla pod

200ml (¾ cup + 1 tablespoon) double cream

½ teaspoon ginger

1 cinnamon stick

In Mary Beaton's 1823 *The Cook and Housekeeper's Complete and Universal Dictionary* in between describing evacuations and exercise was her recipe for Eve's pudding. Traditionally made with apples, replacing them with pears means even less work in the kitchen, as the pears will cook in the base of the pudding without any extra preparation.

I have paired this comforting pudding with my gingerbread custard. The warm, spiced flavours complement the delicate sweetness of the fruit and sponge perfectly.

METHOD

Preheat the oven to 160°C fan (350°F).

Peel, core and chop the pears into large chunks. Place in a bowl and stir together with the butter, lemon juice and sugar. Then transfer to a 20cm x 20cm (8" x 8") oven dish.

For the topping, cream together the butter and sugar until light and fluffy.

Fold in the flour and egg in alternate spoonfuls until blended, then finally add the boiling water to the mix. Spoon the mixture over the pears. Cook in the oven for 30 minutes until the topping is golden.

Meanwhile, in a bowl, whisk together the egg yolks, sugar and cornflour as you start to make the custard.

Pour the milk into a pan and add the split vanilla pod and its seeds, along with the double cream, ginger and the cinnamon stick until it just reaches simmering point. Remove the cinnamon stick.

Pour out a wee bit of the hot milk onto the egg mixture, whisking continuously. Whisk in the rest of the hot milk until well combined, then return to the pan.

Return to a low heat, stirring, until the custard thickens enough to coat the spoon.

Now serve the custard as a topping for your delicious Pear Eve's Pudding.

CNOC NAN UAN

As I reach the top of Cnoc nan Uan, I turn to look across the town of Stornoway, its busy streets, imposing neo-gothic castle and cars driving in from the villages across the island. Beside me, a towering monument reaches for the heavens, solemn and steadfast, dedicated as a memorial to the men of Lewis who lost their lives in the First World War.

Sunday, 2 August 1914 is a day etched in the memories of the islanders.

As the church doors opened that morning, the men and women of the villages sat solemnly dressed in black, the minister stepped into their church pulpit with a message voiced with a mix of trepidation and urgency. Instead of sharing his verses of solace and salvation from the Bible, he delivered a solemn proclamation from the Royal Navy announcing the mobilisation of all men trained with arms to be ready to go to war.

As the sermon was hurriedly read and prayers called, a sea of women sat with heads bowed, their faces concealed beneath hats, clutching tightly onto their handkerchiefs, their hearts heavy with worry and fear. The island, which had felt shielded against what was going on in the world, now found itself grappling with the harsh realities of war. As the church emptied its pews, an extra-ordinary commotion unfolded, shattering the tranquillity that typically embraced the Sabbath on the island.

That afternoon, motor cars were dispatched to all parts of the island with notices summoning the men to report themselves to Stornoway by Monday morning. Customs officers and police visited the fishing boats lying at Stornoway and informed all men of the news. Boats were tied up, fishing nets were left on the quayside, the proclamation affected not only every village, but practically every family on the island.

On that fateful Monday morning, the air buzzed with a mixture of anticipation, camaraderie and a tinge of melancholy. As the men boarded the steamers *Claymore* and *Sheila* ready to transport them across the Minch, towards the unknown perils of war, the quayside was thronged with well-wishers. Amid the deafening din, heartfelt wishes and fervent prayers were exchanged as the men bid farewell to loved ones.

Slowly but surely, as the steamers navigated their way past Arnish, the clamour of voices and the echoes of tearful farewells gradually faded, leaving behind a poignant silence that settled heavy upon the hearts of those left behind. The weight of reality lingered, an unspoken reminder of the uncertain days that lay ahead and the profound absence that now marked their lives.

The first Lewisman lost was a nineteen-year-old seaman Kenneth John MacLeod, Royal Naval Reserve. He was killed in action on 14 September 1914, during a battle between HMS *Carmania* and the German auxiliary cruiser *Cap Trafalgar* in the South Atlantic.

Week after week, the pages of the *Stornoway Gazette* were filled with sombre announcements, recounting tales of loss and tragedy that resonated deeply within the community. With heavy hearts, the islanders braced themselves for the names and stories that awaited them, their souls weighed down by the ever-mounting casualties and the cruel grip of uncertainty. At the end of May 1916, news was received that, during the Battle of Jutland, eleven Lewismen were lost in the sinking of HMS *Invincible*.

Kenneth John MacLeod was the first of 1,151 men out of 6,712 who died in battle. On an island with a population of just over 29,000 men, women and children, life on the island would never be the same again.

Back home, helping on his father's croft in the village of Balallan when the news of the mobilisation was announced, Malcolm Martin was called up to join the Royal Naval Reserve. He had been working as a shepherd in Punta Arenas in Chile, but had returned home for a visit just as war broke out. Like many men, he appealed the call-up. His father Neil wrote a letter supported by sixteen of his neighbours requesting an exemption due to his mother's poor health and saying that if he were to be called away, croft work, cattle and sheep would go unattended and the annual supply of peat to keep the house warm would be left uncut. The tribunal rejected his appeal, and he was requested to join HMS *Pembroke*.

After surviving the war, Malcolm Martin joined hundreds of Lewismen on their long journey home. They had arrived by rail at Kyle of Lochalsh on the western Highlands mainland and were looking forward to catching the steam ferry home. The regular ferry, the SS *Sheila*, was soon packed, so the Royal Navy ordered the *Iolaire* across the Minch to carry the extra men left behind.

On 31 December 1918, he boarded the HMY *Iolaire* bound for Stornoway. The boat was packed with naval reservists and merchant seamen who had survived the war. Brothers met brothers, cousins met cousins and neighbours met neighbours for the first time since leaving the island over four years before.

Making its final approach into Stornoway on a dark night and in a strong gale, the *Iolaire* changed course at the wrong point. At 1.55 a.m. on New Year's Day, the boat hit the rocks near the village of Holm, a mere twenty yards from the shore of the Isle of Lewis and less than a mile from the safe harbour of Stornoway.

With 280 men crowded onboard, the boat began to sink in the storm. Men drowned as they jumped into the sea and were dashed against jagged rocks. By the time the first New Year's Day of peacetime dawned, 201 men had lost their lives, among them 174 Lewismen, including Malcolm Martin, and seven Harrismen, on the very shores of the island they called home.

It was the most tragic single event to hit Lewis and Harris, and one of the worst maritime disasters of the twentieth century. Some thirty-nine MacLeods, brothers and cousins, were drowned. It is believed this is the highest number of seamen bearing the same surname ever drowned on the same naval ship in Europe. The unimaginable grief that the island suffered as a consequence of the tragedy has had an intense and lasting effect.

The echoes of the war reverberated

through the islands, triggering another chapter of emigration. Many of those who had served overseas had been promised crofting land on their return, but were met with a harsh reality. Prime Minister Stanley Baldwin urged these men to seek their fortunes overseas instead, in distant colonies. In the wake of this shattered promise, an exodus unfolded, leaving a profound mark on the land.

In the early 1920s, a staggering 3,000 individuals from Lewis alone embarked on journeys to Canada, America and further afield, compounding the aftermath of war and casting a sombre shadow over the island.

Among the vessels that etched their names in the annals of departure was the *Metagama*. The SS *Metagama* was a Canadian Pacific Railway steamship. Just over one hundred years ago on Saturday, 21 April 1923, she sailed from Stornoway with three hundred young Lewis emigrants on board.

So, as I stand on top of Cnoc nan Uan watching island life go by, I can't help but sense the enduring spirit of the people of Lewis. Though the scars of our history are still etched upon our collective memory, they serve as a testament to our strength. We carry the weight of the past with grace, knowing that it has shaped us into who we are today.

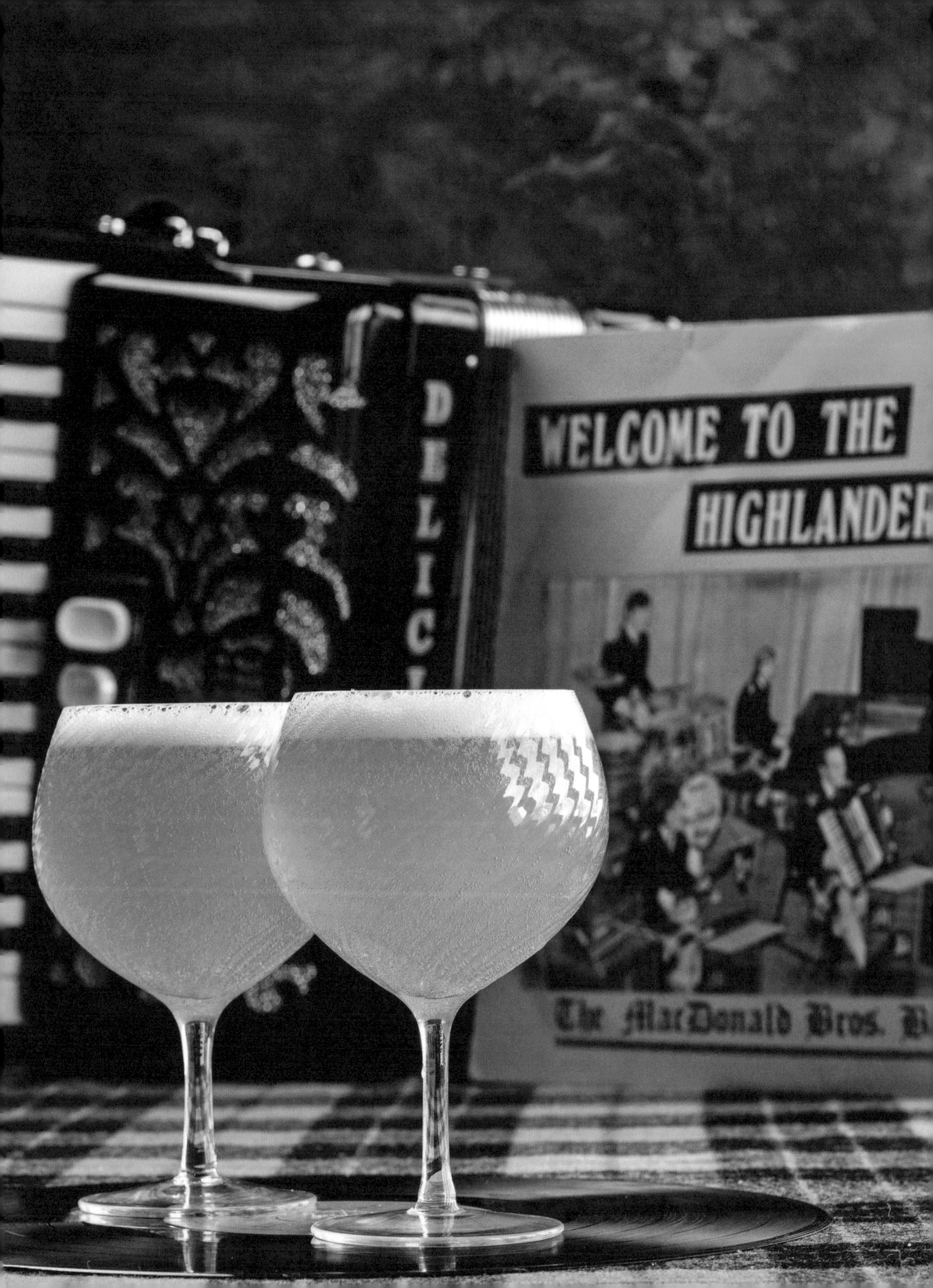
WELCOME TO THE
HIGHLANDER
The MacDonald Bros.

THE MACLEOD

MAKES 1 SERVING

INGREDIENTS

50ml (3 tablespoons +
1 teaspoon) whisky
(I recommend Jura Pale
Ale Cask)

½ a lemon, juiced, plus a
slice for garnish

150ml (½ cup +
2 tablespoons) wheat
beer, chilled

150ml (½ cup +
2 tablespoons) cloudy
lemonade, chilled

When you search the Scottish Register of Tartans, there are currently 24 official MacLeod tartans, from MacLeod of Raasay to MacLeod of Argentina. But there's no doubt which MacLeod tartan is the most recognisable – the Loud MacLeod! Wearing the MacLeod of Lewis is a surefire way to stand out.

To celebrate MacLeods across the world, I've created this cocktail that'll keep you dancing all night at the cèilidh!

METHOD

In a Copa or pilsner glass, add the whisky, lemon juice, wheat beer and top with your cloudy lemonade.

Garnish with a slice of lemon.

THE PARK BAR DRAM

MAKES 1 SERVING

INGREDIENTS

For the garnish

2 tablespoons grapefruit juice

Fine sea salt

For the cocktail

50ml (3 tablespoons + 1 teaspoon) gin

50ml (3 tablespoons + 1 teaspoon) grapefruit juice

A few drops of Angostura bitters

25ml (1 tablespoon + 2 teaspoons) sparkling lemonade (or enough to top up the glass)

Opened in 1895, the Park Bar is the beating heart of Glasgow's Gaelic community. This lively establishment has been hosting cèilidh nights for well over 50 years, providing a home for Scotland's most talented traditional musicians to fill the pub with tunes every weekend.

When I moved to university in Glasgow in the early 1990s, I got a job behind the bar and absolutely loved it. Today, the Park Bar continues to thrive under the guidance of sisters Nina and Winnie, who carry on the tradition of offering a warm and inviting atmosphere to all who step through the door.

So, if you find yourself in Glasgow, don't miss the opportunity to pay a visit – and order yourself the Park Bar Dram!

METHOD

Dip the rim of a tumbler into a saucer of grapefruit juice, then into a saucer of salt, just to get a light coating. Fill the glass with ice and add the gin and grapefruit juice. Next, a couple of dashes of Angostura bitters and finally top with sparking lemonade.

THE TARBERT

MAKES 4 SERVINGS

INGREDIENTS

For the syrup

400g (14oz) rhubarb

250g (9oz) sugar

1 teaspoon vanilla bean
   paste

500ml (2 cups) water

For the cocktail

200ml (¾ cup +
   1 tablespoon) gin

50ml (3 tablespoons +
   1 teaspoon) lime juice
   (about 2 limes)

I'm serving you up a classic gimlet cocktail, where the stars of the show are definitely the vibrant pink of the rhubarb syrup and the Harris Gin. The tartness of rhubarb is an exquisite complement to the botanical notes of the gin. And the best part is, we grow the main ingredient right in our garden! This also works well as a tall drink, so you can top with prosecco or sparkling lemonade for a bit of fizz.

METHOD

Chop the rhubarb into small chunks, add the sugar, vanilla and water, bring to a boil and simmer for 20 minutes. Strain through a sieve into a jug and leave to cool.

Fill a cocktail shaker with ice cubes. To make 2 cocktails, add 100ml (⅓ cup + 2 tablespoons) of your rhubarb syrup, half of the gin and half of the freshly squeezed lime juice. Shake until well chilled, then strain the cocktail into 2 martini glasses. Repeat when you are ready for another!

Oh, and keep the sweet rhubarb purée to stir into your porridge for breakfast the next morning.

WHISKY GALORE

MAKES 1 SERVING

INGREDIENTS

25ml (1 tablespoon +
    2 teaspoons) whisky

25ml (1 tablespoon +
    2 teaspoons) Aperol

Tonic water (Fever-Tree
    Mediterranean works well)

Orange wedge, to garnish

In 1941, when the SS *Politician*, bound for America, was blown off course and came aground on the rocks of Eriskay. People came from as far as the Isle of Lewis to battle the waves and 'rescue' the 260,000 bottles of whisky that the ship had been carrying.

The police then began raiding villages and crofts, with the whisky rescuers being arrested, fined and even, in some cases, jailed. It's estimated that 24,000 bottles were either hidden, destroyed or drunk by the residents of the Outer Hebrides.

Ramsey's granny Catrìona was born and raised on Eriskay and he has spent nearly every summer back on the island. His cocktail is the perfect serve to sup while reading the classic Compton Mackenzie novel *Whisky Galore!*

METHOD

Add the whisky and Aperol to an ice-filled glass, then top up with tonic water. Mix and garnish with a fresh orange wedge.

HOT, DARK & STORMY

INGREDIENTS

For the ginger tea

250ml (1 cup) water

1 teabag ginger tea

3 whole cloves

3cm (1") of fresh ginger,
   peeled and grated

1 teaspoon honey

For the cocktail

50ml (3 tablespoons +
   1 teaspoon) dark rum

Lime wedges

Fresh nutmeg, grated

Whether you've snuggled up on your favourite chair by the stove, or settled around a bonfire on the shoreline, a warming mug of tea with a boozy kick will keep the winter chill at bay. This has all the flavours of a classic Dark & Stormy, but is infused with fresh ginger, cloves and honey. I can't wait for winter!

METHOD

To make the tea, pour the water into a saucepan and add the teabag and cloves. Bring to a simmer and add the grated ginger and honey. After 5 minutes take it off the heat, strain until you are left with just the freshly brewed tea.

Into a mug, pour in the rum and top with the hot ginger tea. Squeeze in the lime wedges and dust with nutmeg. Serve and get cosy.

SHONA'S HARRIS GIN MARGARITA

MAKES 2 SERVINGS

INGREDIENTS

120ml (½ cup) Harris Gin

60ml (¼ cup) Triple Sec

60ml (¼ cup) lime juice, plus a slice to garnish

30ml (¼ cup) sugar syrup

3 to 4 shakes of Angostura bitters

Salt and sugar, for salting the glass rim

When the Isle of Harris Distillery opened its doors in 2015, Shona MacLeod was the first to welcome guests through the door. Born and raised in the village of Tarbert, where the Distillery calls home, Shona is the Distillery Blender and a pretty good cocktail maker!

One of her standout creations is a unique twist on the classic Margarita, which showcases the distinctive flavour of Harris Gin in place of the traditional tequila. This refreshing and captivating cocktail offers a delightful fusion of island botanicals, adding a touch of Hebridean charm to this classic drink.

METHOD

Salt the rim of your favourite glass with 50/50 salt and sugar. For a special treat, use Cool Chile Co. Sweet Hibiscus Rim, which has salt, sugar, chilli flakes and dried hibiscus.

Shake all the ingredients in a cocktail shaker over lots of ice until really chilled on the outside of the shaker. Strain into the glass and garnish with a slice of lime on the rim.

THE ISLANDER

MAKES 2 SERVINGS

INGREDIENTS

100ml (⅓ cup +
   2 tablespoons) whisky
   (I recommend a Jura
   Bourbon Cask)

50ml (3 tablespoons +
   1 teaspoon) pineapple
   juice

50g (1¾oz) apricot jam

50ml (3 tablespoons +
   1 teaspoon) freshly
   squeezed lemon juice

Sprig of thyme to garnish

When Andy, the Brand Ambassador at Jura Whisky, offers to craft a cocktail – well, it's impossible to turn him down!

With his passion for whisky, he has created the Islander cocktail. This combines the smoothness of Jura whisky with the tropical notes of pineapple juice, a touch of sweetness from apricot jam and sourness from the lemon. This whisky cocktail will undoubtedly make you feel like an islander!

METHOD

Add the whisky, pineapple juice, apricot jam and lemon juice into a cocktail shaker and stir until the jam has combined with the other ingredients. Fill the shaker with ice and shake for about 15 seconds until perfectly chilled.

Fine strain into your glass over cubed ice and garnish with a sprig of thyme.

HÒRO GHEALLAIDH COCKTAIL

MAKES 4 SERVINGS

INGREDIENTS

For the mincemeat syrup

150ml (½ cup +
   2 tablespoons) water

150g (5oz) sugar

90g (3oz) mincemeat

For the cocktails

2 tablespoons mincemeat

200ml (¾ cup +
   1 tablespoon) gin

100ml (⅓ cup +
   2 tablespoons) dry
   vermouth

100ml (⅓ cup +
   2 tablespoons) cloudy
   apple juice

Hòro Gheallaidh is the Gaelic for a shindig or a big party and this Christmas cocktail is guaranteed to get you into the festive spirit!

Inspired by the flavours of the fruit and spices found in mincemeat, a special syrup is created and shaken together with gin, vermouth and apple juice. The result is a harmonious blend of seasonal aromas and flavours, capturing the essence of Christmas in each sip.

Oh, and if you're in need of a mincemeat recipe, be sure to check out *The Hebridean Baker: Recipes and Wee Stories from the Scottish Islands* for inspiration. Nollaig Chridheil!

METHOD

To make the syrup, add the water, sugar and mincemeat into a pan and bring to a simmering boil for 2 minutes. Strain through a muslin cloth and allow to cool.

To make the cocktail, muddle the mincemeat in a cocktail shaker, then add the gin, dry vermouth, cloudy apple juice, 120ml (½ cup) of the mincemeat syrup and a handful of ice. Shake well until cold, then fine strain into martini glasses. Garnish – perhaps with a twist of orange for a festive feel.

An uair a bhios an deoch a-staigh, bidh an ciall a mach!

WHEN THE DRINK'S IN, THE WIT'S OOT!

TAKE YOUR PARTNERS

'Take your partners for a Highland Schottische!' announces Archie, the cèilidh band caller.

The sound of chairs scraping back, the clinking of drams settling on tables, and the eager acceptance of dance invitations all get drowned out as the band begin to tune their instruments.

As I stand facing my dance partner, Catriona, the billowing sound of the accordion introduces the tune to whoops from around the hall. As the melody begins, our feet skip and propel us forward to the beat of the music. The steps repeated before a whirlwind of pas-de-basque take us back round to begin the dance again. Is it just me, or is the Highland Schottische getting more tiring as every year goes by? There's no doubt every cèilidh dancer in the land has exclaimed '*again?!*' as the band start up yet another set of Brochan Lom just when you think the dance is over!

As the fiddle's bow draws out the last note and the accordion releases the final resounding chord, the room erupts in applause. Catriona and I hug, our hearts filled with laughter as we head back to our table to finish that dram.

When you think of a cèilidh dance, it conjures visions of folk being spun around, their kilts and sporrans weaving seamlessly through intricate formations, steps perfectly synchronised, with each stomp of a dancer's foot celebrated by the guests around the dancefloor. Oh, and did I mention the whisky?

Originally known as the Balmoral Schottische, the Highland Schottische was first danced in the 1850s and was soon joined by another regular – the Dashing White Sergeant. This reel gathers you into threes and is one of my firm favourites.

A group of six people join hands in a circle and dance clockwise and anticlockwise for eight beats each. The group then split into two, at which point the person in the middle does a set to the person on their right and then spins them. Then repeating this with the person on their left before spinning both two times.

The group then hold hands, face the other set of three and move towards each other, stamping their feet in the middle and then going backwards, finishing off with a clap of their hands, as you walk through to be joined by a new set of three!

Nowadays, these dances along with a Military Two-Step, Gay Gordons (named after the Gordon Highlanders army regiment), St Bernard's Waltz, Canadian Barn Dance and an Eightsome Reel will be wearing out the dancefloors of village halls across Scotland every Friday and Saturday night. But in the 1960s, if you couldn't make it to a cèilidh,

you could settle down on the sofa and watch one on television.

At 6.20 every Saturday night on BBC in the early 1960s, Andy Stewart would welcome the audience to *The White Heather Club*.

'Come in, come in, it's nice tae see ye
How's yerself? Ye're looking grand.
Tak yer ease we'll try to please ye
Man ye're welcome, here's my hand!'

These are the words he sang at the start of each show to an audience of over ten million around the country. The half-hour live programme would feature Andy singing traditional Scottish tunes, a resident troupe of country dancers and the best cèilidh bands of the day.

The show boasted a roster of Scottish entertainers, the crème de la crème of their time. Renowned names like Jimmy Shand, Bobby MacLeod and James Urquhart graced the screen as regular performers. And the skilled footwork of resident dancers Dixie Ingram and Isobel James added an extra layer of charm to the performances. Such was the immense popularity of the show that it sparked numerous stage adaptations throughout the years. Esteemed stars such as Kenneth McKellar and Moira Anderson, already firmly established in their own right, took centre stage and joined Andy Stewart in these productions.

The celebration of Scottish music and dance has always extended far beyond the borders of Scotland itself. From the bustling cities of the United States to South Island, New Zealand, I have seen Scottish communities flourish, preserving and celebrating their heritage with unwavering pride.

It had always been a dream of mine to visit Cape Breton Island, which is nestled on the Atlantic coast of the Canadian province of Nova Scotia. Thousands of Hebridean folk settled there during the eighteenth and nineteenth centuries and, to this day, its parish halls, pubs and many homes are still filled with the sound of traditional Scottish and Gaelic tunes.

The music scene on the island is second to none, and on my first day there, my guides Adam Hill and Amy Beaton took me to the Celtic Music Interpretive Centre in Judique. I thought, before heading out onto the Cèilidh Trail, it would be best to learn the differences between the MacIsaacs and the MacMasters and be able to name at least a Rankin or two!

That evening we headed to the famous Red Shoe Pub in Mabou. There, as I was getting served at the bar, two folk were standing beside me speaking Gaelic – and I found out they were from South Uist.

'Oh, I see you're singing at the cèilidh tonight?' said the barman as we chatted.

'I am?' I said, bemused as he passed me the programme with my name appearing on the bill.

'Ahh, we forgot to tell you!' said Adam, smiling apologetically.

I took a long drink from my glass; Dutch courage before we took the short walk across the road to find every seat in the community hall taken.

After a set of Cape Breton step dancing, I got on stage to sing a couple of Gaelic tunes. I felt quite emotional that I was over 2,500 miles from home and folk were singing along in Gaelic to the choruses I sang.

Perched upon the hills in Iona, overlooking the Bras d'Or Lake, we visited Baile nan Gàidheal, the Highland Village, North America's only living history museum for Gaelic language and culture. Stepping into a blackhouse and farmhouses, similar to those that many immigrants from the islands would have called home, I found demonstrations on weaving, waulking the tweed and I even got served some homemade white pudding! It made Cape Breton feel like a home away from home.

In between the communities of Christmas Island, Whycocomagh, Grand Narrows and West Bay are the villages of Oban, New Harris, Dingwall and Dundee. I was constantly stopping the car to take pictures of myself by the road signs! But that evening I was on my way to Inverness County. Famous for its square dances at Glencoe Mills Hall.

As I stepped through the door, the dancefloor was already full. I sat there with my foot tapping, trying to understand the formations, but there wasn't time – I was whisked onto the dancefloor. And though it took me a few sets to get the moves, the regulars soon began reeling me in the right direction! Cape Breton really is a special place and I hope I get to return soon, perhaps next time for Celtic Colours, their international music festival hosted every October.

So, it doesn't matter if you're in Scotland, Canada, Australia, New Zealand or the US, it's easy to find a kindred spirit. One to share your love of Gaelic music, cèilidh dancing or just supping a dram. Let's continue to celebrate our amazing culture, on and off the dancefloor. Now, who's up for a Strip the Willow?

MORNING ROLLS WITH LORNE SAUSAGE

MAKES 9

INGREDIENTS

For the Lorne sausage

100g (3½oz) pancetta

750g (1lb 10½oz) beef mince

2 tablespoons salt

½ tablespoon ground nutmeg

½ tablespoon coriander

¼ tablespoon smoked paprika

1 tablespoon ground black pepper

200g (7oz) water

150g (5oz) panko breadcrumbs

For the morning rolls

7g (¼oz) yeast

2 teaspoons sugar

500ml (2 cups) lukewarm water

800g (1lb 12oz) strong bread flour

2 teaspoons salt

50g (1¾oz) lard, cubed

Semolina powder for dusting

This recipe is dedicated to all the Scots around the world who are longing for a taste of home. One thing that's often mentioned when I ask people what they miss about Scotland is the simple pleasure of heading down to the local shop on a weekend for fresh morning rolls and Lorne sausage. It's a truly heavenly combination that holds a special place in our hearts. So, let's bring a slice of Scotland to your kitchen and recreate this iconic pairing that will transport you back home! Just don't forget to start your preparation the day before, as the Lorne sausage needs to chill overnight.

METHOD

To make the Lorne sausage

Line a 2lb (900g) loaf tin with baking parchment and set it aside.

Blitz the pancetta in a food processor and add to a bowl along with the mince, salt, nutmeg, coriander, smoked paprika and black pepper.

Slowly add the water and mix into a sticky consistency. Add the breadcrumbs and stir in evenly. Pack this mixture into the prepared loaf tin, cover with clingfilm and place in the fridge to set overnight.

The next morning, when the sausage has set, and you have made your rolls, slice into 1cm (½") slices. Grill or fry for 3 minutes each side.

To make the morning rolls

Dissolve the yeast and sugar in the lukewarm water and put it to one side. Sieve the flour and salt into a bowl and, with your fingertips, rub the lard into the flour until it becomes like fine breadcrumbs.

Pour in your liquid and mix it into a dough, then knead for 15 minutes. Roll in the semolina powder and leave to rise for an hour or until it's doubled in size.

Punch back the dough, shape into 9 rolls, flatten a little with your hand and sprinkle on more semolina. Leave to prove, covered, for another hour on a baking tray.

Preheat your oven to 210°C fan (450°F) and bake for 15 minutes. Serve with a slice or two of Lorne sausage and your favourite breakfast additions!

THE CÈILIDH SCONES

MAKES 6

INGREDIENTS

275g (10oz) self-raising flour

1 teaspoon baking powder

½ teaspoon mustard powder

75g (2½oz) butter, chilled and cubed

100g (3½oz) pickle (Branston's small chunk pickle works well)

120g (4¼oz) Cheddar, grated

1 egg, beaten

50g (1¾oz) milk, plus extra to brush

Pinch of salt

Cèilidhs have been a traditional custom over the years in the homes and villages of the islands. Young and old would gather together for a night of storytelling, poems, songs. And often, if someone in the village had an accordion, that would be brought along too. Food would be served and maybe even a couple of drams of whisky.

If you are planning your own cèilidh, these scones would be perfect to serve. I just hope your accordion playing is better than mine!

METHOD

Preheat the oven to 180°C (400°F).

Mix the flour, baking powder, mustard powder and a large pinch of salt in a bowl. Rub in the butter using your fingertips, until the mixture resembles breadcrumbs. Add the pickle and 100g (3½oz) of grated Cheddar, then mix with a knife until combined.

Make a well in the centre of the mixture, add the beaten egg and milk and stir everything together. Knead briefly in the bowl until the dough just comes together.

Tip your dough out on a lightly floured surface, pat out to an even 3cm (1¼") thickness. Stamp into rounds, transfer to a baking sheet dusted in flour and brush tops lightly with milk and sprinkle the remaining Cheddar on top.

Bake for 20 minutes until golden and risen. Transfer to a wire rack to cool slightly. Serve warm with salted butter or with mustard, ham, pickled onions and salad leaves.

BAKED POTATO COTTAGE PIES

SERVES 6

INGREDIENTS

6 large baked potatoes

75g (2½oz) butter

75ml (⅓ cup) double cream

100g (3½oz) mature
    Cheddar, grated

Oil, to bake the potatoes

Salt and pepper, to season

For the cottage pie filling

1 large onion, chopped

2 sticks celery, chopped

650g (1lb 6¾oz) beef
    mince

2 tablespoons tomato purée

Splash of Worcestershire
    sauce

1 tablespoon plain flour

150ml (½ cup +
    2 tablespoons) red wine

4 sprigs fresh thyme, leaves
    only

400ml (1⅔ cup) beef stock

Olive oil, for frying

Salt and ground black
    pepper

If you're like me and have a deep love for classic comfort dishes like mince & tatties, cottage pie and shepherd's pie, you'll love this lunchtime-friendly version that is as delicious as it is satisfying. Instead of the usual potato crust, we've served a perfectly baked potato as the vessel for our tasty mince.

Each potato becomes an individual serving, beautifully presented and inviting you to dig in, making it the perfect midday meal.

METHOD

Preheat the oven to 170°C fan (375°F).

Rub a little oil and seasoning over the potatoes, then bake on a baking sheet for 60 to 75 minutes until the flesh is tender and the skin crisp and golden.

Meanwhile, make the filling. Add the onion and celery to some olive oil in a large pan and cook until softened.

In another pan, cook the mince until browned and any water has evaporated. Stir the mince into the onion and celery when ready.

Add the tomato purée and Worcestershire sauce and cook for 1 minute. Stir in the flour and cook for a further minute. Pour in the red wine and add the thyme leaves.

Add the stock and simmer for an hour until the mixture has thickened. You can also make this ahead of time and warm before assembling.

To serve

When the potatoes are cooked but cool enough to handle, slice a thin portion off the top of each potato. Carefully scoop out most of the inside of each potato and transfer to a bowl.

Add the butter and cream to the potatoes in the bowl, then mash well. Stir in the cheese until well combined. Season with salt and pepper to taste.

Keep the oven at 170°C fan (375°F).

Place the hollowed-out potatoes on a baking sheet and fill each potato to the brim with the mince. Now top each one with a scoop of mashed potato.

Bake for 10 to 12 minutes until the cheese has melted and the potato topping is slightly browned. Serve with a fresh green salad.

PETER'S SCOTCH BROTH

SERVES 6

INGREDIENTS

2 carrots

2 turnips

2 potatoes

2 celery stalks, chopped

2 onions, chopped

1kg (2lb 3oz) lamb shoulder

2 litres (2 quarts) cold water

2 bay leaves

75g (2½oz) pearl barley

Salt and ground black
  pepper, to season

Olive oil, to sauté

Us Scots, we do soup well! Cock-a-Leekie, Cullen Skink and Pea & Ham are all classics, but once you've learned how to make a Scotch broth, life is sure to be inherently better forever. Comforting, hearty and filled with goodness, Maria Rundell put Scotch broth into print in 1805 when, at the age of 60 she released her first cookbook, *A New System of Domestic Cookery*, which sold over half a million copies.

I wonder if Peter's version will help sell as many copies of this cookbook?

METHOD

Cut the carrots, turnips, potatoes and celery into equal 2.5cm (1") squares.

Sauté the onions and celery with some olive oil in a pan.

Meanwhile, place the lamb in a large soup pan, cover with the cold water and bring to a simmer. Add the onion, celery and bay leaves to the pan. Allow to simmer, then add the pearl barley and cook for an hour.

Add the carrots, turnips and potatoes to the pan. Season well. Simmer for an hour.

Take the lamb out of the pot and slice the meat into bitesize chunks, then place back into the pan.

Serve a hearty portion into a big bowl, perhaps with some crusty bread and butter, and enjoy this broth's hearty, cosy goodness.

BRADAN BURGERS WITH HOMEMADE COLESLAW

MAKES 4 BURGERS

INGREDIENTS

For the burgers

2 thick slices of stale white bread, crusts removed

750g (1lb 10½oz) salmon fillets

3 spring onions, trimmed and chopped

2 tablespoons dill, chopped

1 lemon, zested

1 egg white

3½ tablespoons vegetable oil

Salt and freshly ground black pepper, to season

Burger buns, to serve

For the coleslaw

½ red or white cabbage, shredded

1 red onion, finely sliced

1 carrot, grated

1 tablespoon chives, chopped

3 tablespoons mayonnaise

2 satsumas, juiced

1 tablespoon wholegrain mustard

Salt and freshly ground black pepper, to season

Peter's dad Graham has spent his life out at sea, and I know that he would love these salmon burgers served with his homemade coleslaw. This recipe makes a perfect alternative to beef with the zesty lemon, aromatic dill and the subtle crunch of spring onions creating a burst of freshness to the salmon.

To complete the burger, Graham's homemade coleslaw takes centre stage. Crisp cabbage, crunchy carrots, red onion and a tangy satsuma-infused dressing superbly complements the flavours of the salmon. Who needs McDonald's when you have the MacQueens!

METHOD

In a food processor, blitz the bread into crumbs. Remove the skin from the salmon and cut into chunks. Add to the processor along with the spring onions, dill, lemon zest and egg white, then blitz until just combined.

Season the salmon mixture well and divide into 4 portions. Shape each into a burger. Cover and chill for 30 minutes.

Meanwhile, prepare your coleslaw. Put the cabbage, onion, carrot and chives into a bowl.

In another bowl, mix together the mayonnaise, juice from the satsumas and the wholegrain mustard. Season with salt and freshly ground black pepper and stir to thoroughly combine. Pour this dressing over the vegetables and toss to create your coleslaw.

Now heat some vegetable oil in a large nonstick pan over a medium heat and fry your chilled salmon burgers for 3 to 4 minutes on each side, or until golden brown all over and completely cooked through.

Serve in a burger bun with your favourite accompaniments.

MARMALADE CHICKEN

SERVES 4

INGREDIENTS

4 tablespoons marmalade

35ml (2 tablespoons + 1 teaspoon) freshly squeezed orange juice

2 teaspoons Dijon mustard

1 tablespoon olive oil

750g (1lb 10½oz) boneless chicken thighs

Marmalade is the perfect alternative to honey to make a sticky, sweet, zesty glaze for a roast chicken. All the work is done by the marinade, making this a perfect hassle-free midweek meal.

METHOD

Combine the marmalade with the orange juice, mustard and olive oil. Coat the chicken thighs all over, then cover and marinate in the fridge for at least 30 minutes.

Preheat the oven to 170°C fan (375°F).

Place the marinated chicken into a baking dish, cover with foil and bake for 15 minutes.

Remove the foil and cook for another 30 minutes, until the thighs are golden and caramelised, and the marinade has thickened.

Serve with mashed potato and green veg.

Is e iomadaidh nan làmh a nì an obair aotrom.

MANY HANDS MAKE LIGHT WORK.

WHISKY FONDUE

SERVES 4

INGREDIENTS

2 banana shallots

2 tablespoons butter

250ml (1 cup) chicken stock

250g (9oz) Emmental

250g (9oz) Gruyère

250g (9oz) Brie

20g (¾oz) cornflour

50ml (3 tablespoons +
   1 teaspoon) whisky

Freshly ground pepper

When I appeared on the Canadian TV show *The Social*, I met chef and food stylist Sandra Watson.

'I think I have a recipe you might like,' said Sandra as we sat talking food after the show. When she told me about her whisky fondue, I knew it would become a regular dish back home on the island. The warmth of the whisky complements the strong cheese flavours and the caramelised shallots bring the perfect sweetness to the dish. Thank you, Sandra!

METHOD

Chop the shallots lengthwise and fry in the butter over a low heat for about 20 minutes until golden brown.

Pour the chicken stock into a Dutch oven and bring to a gentle simmer.

In a bowl, grate your Emmental and Gruyère cheeses, remove the rind of the Brie, slice into cubes and sprinkle the cornflour on top and coat thoroughly.

Stir the cheese into the stock in batches until the cheese has melted and the fondue is smooth; you can add more stock if needed.

Stir in the whisky and caramelised shallots, grind in some pepper and serve in a fondue pot with baby potatoes, crusty bread and pickled vegetables.

CHARLIE BARLEY'S MEATBALLS

SERVES 4

INGREDIENTS

For the tomato sauce

6 shallots, roughly chopped

2 sticks celery, chopped

2 teaspoons dried thyme

2 garlic cloves, finely chopped

4 tins plum tomatoes

300ml (1¼ cup) water

2 tablespoons tomato purée

2 teaspoons Worcestershire sauce

2 teaspoons salt

1 teaspoon freshly ground pepper

Olive oil, to sauté

For the meatballs

250g (9oz) Stornoway Black Pudding

500g (1lb 2oz) minced beef

100g (3½oz) pancetta, finely chopped

2 tablespoons chopped parsley, plus extra to serve

1 teaspoon dried thyme

2 tablespoons panko breadcrumbs

50g (1¾oz) Parmesan, grated

2 eggs

2 teaspoons sea salt flakes

1 teaspoon freshly ground black pepper

I was on a radio show recently and the host was chatting to me about my recipes and life on the islands.

'If I was to visit Lewis, what is the first thing I should do when I arrive in Stornoway?' he asked. Without a pause, I replied, 'Go to Charles Macleod butcher's and pick up a black pudding!'

I serve Charlie Barley's black pudding for breakfast, lunch and dinner – but this could be one of my favourite recipes. Serving a little bit of Italy in the Hebrides!

METHOD

First, make the sauce. Sauté the shallots and celery in olive oil until they begin to soften. Stir in the thyme and garlic. Add the tomatoes and water and stir in along with the tomato purée, Worcestershire sauce, salt and pepper, then simmer for an hour.

To make the meatballs, start by crumbling the black pudding and mince into a bowl. Add the pancetta, parsley, thyme, breadcrumbs, Parmesan, eggs, salt and pepper. Mix this all together with your hands.

Make roughly 32 golf ball-sized meatballs, place them on a board and chill them in the fridge for about 30 minutes.

Once chilled, stir the meatballs into the sauce and let them simmer for 30 minutes, then allow the pan to rest for 10 minutes off the heat. Sprinkle some parsley on top and serve with pasta or thick slices of your favourite sourdough.

LOCH DUART SALMON WELLINGTON

SERVES 6

INGREDIENTS

75g (2½oz) watercress, chopped

200g (7oz) cream cheese

2 tablespoons fresh dill, chopped

½ a lemon, zested and juiced

2 x 320g (11¼oz) packs of ready-rolled puff pastry

2 x 500g (1lb 2oz) skinless, boneless salmon fillets

2 eggs, yolks only, beaten

Flour, for dusting

Sea salt and freshly ground black pepper, to season

My first weekend job when I was at school was working with my brother Murdo at a salmon farm in Marvig on the Isle of Lewis. Now, when selecting salmon for my kitchen, I always choose Loch Duart salmon. Their salmon are grown in the cold, clear waters of northwest Scotland, giving them a beautiful colour and a firmer texture. This sought-after salmon has graced the world's most discerning tables; it was even served to guests at the royal wedding of Prince William and Catherine Middleton.

And this salmon Wellington, filled with a zingy cream cheese filling and wrapped in a buttery puff pastry, is fit for kings and queens alike!

METHOD

To make the filling, put the watercress, cream cheese, dill, lemon zest and juice into a bowl. Season with sea salt and freshly ground pepper, mix well, then set aside.

Line a baking tray with parchment. Lay a sheet of the puff pastry on the tray so it's 2½cm (1") larger in diameter than the salmon fillet. Place the first of the salmon fillets on the pastry and spread it with a thick layer of the cream cheese mix, then lay the second fillet on top. Brush the edge of the pastry with a little of the beaten yolk, then drape the second sheet of pastry over the salmon and tuck it in at the sides. Trim the edges and press with a fork to seal.

With the leftover pastry, make a fishtail shape and place at one end of the Wellington. Brush with more beaten yolk, then chill in the fridge for 30 minutes.

Using a spoon, create a scale-like effect along the top of the pastry and, with a sharp knife, score lines along the tail. Chill for at least another 30 minutes.

Preheat the oven to 200°C fan (425°F), bake for 20 minutes, lower the heat to 160°C fan (350°F) and bake covered with foil for another 20 minutes more. Rest for 10 minutes before slicing up at the dinner table.

THE WINTER SOLSTICE

What do you buy an islander for Christmas? New yellow wellies? A Stornoway Black Pudding slicer? An eighteen-year-old bottle of whisky, or what about a sleigh to pull Seòras through the snow? Well, all those would normally be perfect under my tree, but this year I'm hoping Santa brings me a torch; yes, a torch. Heading home from a cèilidh, checking the sheep are okay at night or a late-night walk down to the shore hoping *Na Fir-chlis*, the Northern Lights, are dancing in the skies, my torch can go with me everywhere I go. As Christmas Day draws closer and the festive spirit fills the air, the islands of the Hebrides find themselves enveloped in darkness. A short 570 miles from the Arctic Circle, with only a few precious hours of daylight, home fires are kindled in stoves, lamps flicker, casting a golden glow through the windows, welcoming family and neighbours round for a dram.

According to the Stornoway Astronomical Society, the skies above the Outer Hebrides hold the distinction of being the darkest in all of Scotland. None more so than on *Oidhche nan Seachd Suipearan*, the Night of the Seven Suppers. Falling on the 21st of December, it marks *Grian-stad a' Gheamhraidh*, the Winter Solstice, which is the longest night and shortest day of the year. It is so named because it can feel like a night so long that you could sit down to supper seven times before the sun rises again. It's hard to think of anything that would cheer me up more on a dark, stormy evening in the island than the thought of sitting down to seven hearty dishes of food!

In Scotland on the solstice, before the arrival of Christianity, mistletoe that grew on the oak tree was given a blessing. Oaks were seen as sacred, and the winter fruit of the mistletoe was a symbol of life in the dark winter months.

The story is told of Frigga, the Nordic goddess of beauty, who gave birth to her son Baldur on the Winter Solstice. Frigga was so protective of her son, she requested the lands and seas and everything upon them to keep him safe, but she forget to ask one plant.

The jealous god Loki went and found this plant – mistletoe – growing upon a tree. He returned with a branch and cast it at Baldur. The instant it hit, he fell to the ground, dead. Frigga sat by her son and wept; her tears turned into the berries that grow upon the mistletoe. When Frigga placed these berries upon Baldur, he came to life again. And so, Frigga praised the mistletoe as a symbol of love and of peace, and she promised that, forever afterward, whoever stood beneath this plant would be offered a kiss and for ever protected.

It is easy to grow your own mistletoe. Simply take a berry and push it into a crevice in the bark of an apple tree branch. One thing to keep in mind is that mistletoe comes as a male or female plant and, like holly, only the females carry berries. Try and sow a number of seeds in different places to be sure you end up with plants of both. The sticky mistletoe berries are loved by birds such as the thrush, who will spread the seed to new trees.

It has become tradition that, when you kiss someone under the mistletoe, you pick off one of the berries from the branch. Once all the berries have been removed, the kissing has to cease. So, if you're going to hang mistletoe in your house on the Winter Solstice this year, make sure it's a branch loaded with berries!

This is also the perfect night to look up at the dark skies around the Hebrides. The constellation called *An Dreag-bhod*, Little Bear, is home to two stars called *Na Laoigh*, the calves. At the outer end of *An Dreag-bhod* is Polaris, the Pole Star, known in Gaelic as *An Reul-iùil*, the Guiding Star, because of its usefulness to navigators. It hardly moves through the night or year, and always indicates north. And appearing almost as a reversed mirror image of this constellation is the Plough, known as *Crann-arain* in Gaelic, the Baker's Shovel.

Rionnag a' Bhuachaille is the Gaelic name for Venus. When 'the cowherd's star' appeared in the sky, it was time for them to take the cattle home after a day of grazing on the machair.

It wasn't just on *Oidhche nan Seachd Suipearan* that the number seven appeared in Gaelic folklore. Seven is one of the sacred numbers that so frequently occurs in the poems, proverbs and phrases of our people. Instead of having four seasons in one day, we have seven. And for those of you who have

visited the islands, you'd probably agree with the sentiment *Sìde nan Seachd Sian*, the Weather of the Seven Elements!

In legend, there were seven characters that spent the winter in Scotland: they were named the *Seachd Cadalaichean an t-Saoghail*, the Seven Sleepers of the Earth. Namely, *an ialtag*, the bat; *an clacharan*, the stonechat; *an gòbhlan-gaoithe*, the barn swallow; *an t-seilcheag*, the snail; *an dallag*, the dormouse; *an dealan-dè*, the butterfly; and *an seillean*, the bee.

And the number seven even appears in a verse telling of how the belly of a Skye man was so full at the end of his meal:

Seachd sgadain, sàth bradain. Seachd bradain, sàth ròin. Seachd ròin, sàth muice-mara bhig.

Seven herrings, a full meal for a salmon. Seven salmon, a full meal for a seal. Seven seals, a full meal for a wee whale!

The festivities, though, were not just filled with cheer; folklore would sometimes bring a darker side to the season. And there's no doubt the children of Islay were the most well behaved in the build-up to Christmas. This is down to one of the most feared creatures in island stories, not because it brought death, famine or disease but because it stole your Christmas presents!

In the lead-up to Christmas, parents would sternly warn their kids that *Crom Dubh na Nollaig*, the Dark Crooked One of Christmas, could pay them a visit. *Crom Dubh na Nollaig* is often portrayed as a mysterious figure with a crooked staff or a scythe, symbolising the ending of the old year and the coming of the new. How would you know if he was paying you a visit? If screams were heard coming from the roof of your house, that meant the monster was close by and ready to plunder the presents from under your tree. Usually, the noise was that of winter gales whistling down the chimney but why let the truth get in the way of a great story . . .

The incoming winter storms and cold weather on the islands is often predicted by its birdlife. The redwing is a small thrush that visits Scotland in the winter to feast on berry-laden bushes in hedgerows and is known in Gaelic as *Smeòrach an t-Sneachda*, the snow thrush. And it was well known that when a robin, the *Brù-dhearg*, chirped cheerfully of an evening, the next day would bring good weather.

And, on the morning after the Winter Solstice, it is time to celebrate that the days will gradually begin to get longer. Many folk will say *Tha ceum-coilich a' tighinn anns an lath*. The rooster's step – *cois-cheum coilich* – could begin to get slightly longer each day and he would take the hens a wee bit further from the house to feed.

So, despite the darkness of our winters, the Hebrides still has lots to celebrate. The storms may rage outside, but within the walls of our homes, the islanders find comfort in the traditions and spirit of the season.

Nollaig Chridheil! Merry Christmas!

AN ISLAND CHRISTMAS

CHERRY CHRISTMAS CAKE

MAKES 12 SLICES

INGREDIENTS

300g (10½oz) raisins

300g (10½oz) sultanas

175g (6¼oz) dried cherries

175ml (¾ cup) cherry brandy, plus extra for 'feeding' the cake

100g (3½oz) butter

150g (5oz) dark brown muscovado sugar

2 eggs

150g (5oz) plain flour

50g (1¾oz) cornflour

2 tablespoons mixed spice

75g (2½oz) ground almonds

100g (3½oz) dark chocolate, grated

425g (15oz) tin of black cherries in syrup, which should yield about 240g (8½oz) of cherries (keep the syrup)

To decorate the cake

4 tablespoons cherry jam

750g (1lb 10½oz) marzipan

750g (1lb 10½oz) fondant icing

While many folk are out trick-or-treating on Halloween, you'll find me in the kitchen, the dulcet tones of Mariah Carey coming from the record player and my Christmas cake going in the oven. It's the ideal day to begin your festive baking, allowing ample time for the cake to mature. I've added a twist by infusing the rich flavours of dark cherries and chocolate. These indulgent ingredients add a decadent touch to this traditional holiday bake.

METHOD

Add your raisins, sultanas and dried cherries to a bowl and pour over the brandy. Cover and leave to soak overnight at room temperature.

The next day, preheat your oven to 130°C fan (300°F). Grease and line the base and sides of a 20cm (8") round loose-bottomed cake tin with baking parchment. Wrap the outside of the tin with a double layer of parchment, about 3cm (1¼") higher than the cake tin, and secure with string.

In a large bowl, cream the butter and sugar together until light and fluffy. Whisk in the eggs one at a time. Gently fold in the flour, cornflour and mixed spice, followed by the ground almonds and grated chocolate.

In a food processor blitz the drained black cherries, then stir in along with your soaked fruit and 4 tablespoons of the cherry syrup from the tin.

Tip into the prepared tin and bake for 3 hours or until a skewer inserted into the centre comes out clean. Set the cake tin on a wire rack, cover and leave to cool completely before removing from the tin.

When cool, pole holes in your cake with a skewer and brush over a tablespoon of cherry brandy (this is the feed) until it has all soaked in.

Remove the cake from its tin. Wrap fully in parchment paper, double wrap in tin foil and place in a lidded cake tin.

After 10 days, unwrap and feed the cake again. Rewrap, store and repeat the feeding every 10 days.

A week before Christmas, Gently warm the cherry jam in a pan and brush it all over the cake. Roll the marzipan out to a 3mm (⅒") thickness. Use the rolling pin to help you lift the marzipan over the cake and carefully unroll. Ease it down the sides, smooth the surface and trim any excess marzipan.

Then roll out and place the fondant icing in a similar fashion over the marzipan. Make it look as smooth and perfect as you can. Decorate further as you choose, then serve.

THE CAILLEACH

SERVES 8

INGREDIENTS

For the cake

7 eggs, separated into yolks and whites

150g (5oz) sugar

1 teaspoon vanilla bean paste

50g (1¾oz) cocoa powder

For the icing

175g (6¼oz) dark chocolate, chopped

250g (9oz) icing sugar

225g (8oz) butter

1 teaspoon vanilla bean paste

In Gaelic mythology, the Cailleach is the symbolic embodiment of the old woman of winter, the bringer of cold and darkness. Traditionally, on Christmas Eve, it was considered good luck to carve the Cailleach's face onto a log and gather around to witness it burn in the fire. In modern times, the celebration has evolved into a more festive occasion and the baking of the Yule log serves as a commemoration to the Cailleach. Don't forget to leave a slice out for her in thanks for her guardianship during the winter.

METHOD

Preheat the oven to 160°C fan (350°F) and line a Swiss roll tin with baking parchment.

Separate the eggs and in a bowl whisk the egg whites until thick, then add 50g (1¾oz) of the sugar and continue to whisk until stiff peaks appear.

In another bowl, whisk 100g (3½oz) of the sugar along with the egg yolks, this should take a couple of minutes to get creamy. Add the vanilla, sieve in the cocoa powder, then fold in. Fold a large spoonful of the egg whites into this mixture, then continue to fold in the rest until completely combined.

Pour the batter into the Swiss roll tin and bake in the oven for 20 minutes.

Once cooled a little, turn the cake out of the tin onto a piece of baking parchment and cover with a clean tea towel.

Now, for the icing. Break up the chocolate, add half to a bowl and place in the microwave in bursts of 20 seconds until melted, then add the rest of the chocolate and stir until completely melted. Allow to cool.

Sieve your icing sugar into a bowl and whisk in the butter. Add the melted chocolate and vanilla and whisk again until smooth. Spread a thin layer of icing over the sponge, then begin to roll the cake.

Using the baking parchment as support, roll the long side of the cake, making a swirl filled with the chocolate buttercream.

Cut a slice off one end of the cake at an angle and one straight. Then on the side of the log, place the angled slice first then the straight slice connecting to it to create the look of a branch. Smother the log with icing, covering the cut-off ends and any branches. Create a wood-like texture by marking along the length of the log with a fork; be creative.

Dust with icing sugar before seving. Remember a slice for the Cailleach!

CHRISTMAS PROFITEROLE PUDS

MAKES 20

INGREDIENTS

For the profiteroles

125g (4½oz) plain flour

25g (1oz) cocoa

100g (3½oz) butter

2 teaspoons sugar

300ml (1¼ cup) water

3 eggs, beaten

For the filling

300ml (1¼ cup) double cream

2 tablespoons icing sugar

75g (2½oz) unsalted, pistachios, shelled and chopped finely

For the topping

200g (7oz) white chocolate, melted (see page 3 for instructions on how to melt your chocolate)

50g (1¾oz) ready-to-roll green icing

15g (½oz) ready-to-roll red icing

If you're looking for a bite-sized festive treat this Christmas, these pistachio cream-filled profiteroles are guaranteed to bring a smile to everyone's face. They are decorated to resemble wee Christmas puddings, complete with all the festive trimmings. They're the very definition of a Christmas cracker!

METHOD

To make the profiteroles

Sieve the flour and cocoa into a bowl.

Place the butter, sugar and water in a small saucepan and heat until the water just reaches boiling point and the butter has melted. Remove from the heat and add the flour and cocoa and beat the mix with a wooden spoon to form a smooth paste. Return to a gentle heat and stir for a minute so the mix comes away from the sides of the pan.

Remove from the heat again and beat for two minutes with a wooden spoon until the mixture comes together and makes a smooth, thick dough. Once the dough has cooled, add the beaten egg, a little at a time, beating after each addition, until the dough is thick and smooth.

Preheat the oven to 200°C fan (425°F), line a baking tray and sprinkle on a bit of water. (This will create steam as the profiteroles cook in the oven.)

Fill a plain-nozzled piping bag with the dough and pipe into small buns about 5cm (2") in diameter onto the baking tray. Use the back of a warm spoon to smooth the top of each profiterole.

Bake the profiteroles for 20 minutes until puffed and risen, then remove from the oven. Make a hole in the bottom of each one with a skewer then return them to the oven, on their sides, for 10 minutes. Remove from the oven and allow to cool completely on a wire rack.

To make the pistachio cream filling

Whip the cream with the icing sugar until it forms soft peaks and fold in the pistachios. Use a piping bag to fill the cooled profiteroles.

Spoon a little of the melted chocolate over each profiterole and leave them to set in the fridge for 30 minutes.

To decorate, create a leaf shape from the green icing and roll tiny berries from the red icing; use these to top each profiterole so it looks like an irresistible wee Christmas pudding.

CHRISTMAS MERINGUE PIE

SERVES 6

INGREDIENTS

320g (11¼oz) pack of ready-rolled shortcrust pastry

For the clementine filling

50ml (3 tablespoons + 1 teaspoon) lemon juice

50g (1¾oz) cornflour

150g (5oz) golden caster sugar

8 clementines, zested

250ml (1 cup) clementine juice

4 egg yolks

50g (1¾oz) butter

For the meringue topping

4 egg whites

2 teaspoons cornflour

180g (6⅓oz) caster sugar

When Christmas brings you clementines, make a meringue pie! Replacing the classic lemon filling with clementine curd brings a festive feel to this colourful dish.

This pie has just the right combination of tart and sweet flavours. Topped with pillowy peaks of toasted meringue, it is a comforting, zesty and light dessert that will bring joy to your festive celebrations.

METHOD

Line a 20cm (8") loose-bottomed cake tin with the pastry. Chill in the fridge for 20 minutes.

Preheat the oven to 180°C fan (400°F). Cover the pastry with baking paper and baking beans and bake for 20 minutes. Remove the beans and paper and continue to cook for a further 5 minutes until the pastry is golden brown. Remove from the oven and set aside to cool.

In a pan, add the lemon juice, cornflour, sugar, clementine zest and juice into a pan. Stir over a low heat, then cook for 2 minutes until it begins to thicken. Add the egg yolks and butter and continue to whisk until thick, then remove from the heat. Cover loosely with clingfilm pressed onto the surface, then set aside to cool.

Preheat the oven 130°C fan (300°F).

Once it is cooled, spoon the clementine filling into the tart case.

For the topping, whisk the egg whites to stiff peaks in a bowl. Add the cornflour a teaspoon at a time and continue to whisk, before adding the sugar a spoonful at a time, whisking well as you go.

Use a piping bag to pipe the meringue onto the pie filling, starting at the outer edge and working inwards until all the filling is covered. Bake for 20 to 25 minutes until the meringue is lightly golden and crisp. Allow to cool before removing from the cake tin to serve.

FESTIVE TRIFLE

INGREDIENTS

For the marmalade jelly

135g (4¾oz) packet of orange jelly

225ml (8oz) boiling water

2 tablespoons marmalade

225ml (8oz) cold water

1 tablespoon orange liqueur

1 orange, peeled and thinly sliced

For the trifle cake

200g (7oz) sugar

200g (7oz) butter

4 eggs, beaten

200g (7oz) self-raising flour

1 teaspoon baking powder

2 tablespoons milk

For the custard

6 large egg yolks

2 tablespoons sugar

2 tablespoons cornflour

2½ teaspoons vanilla bean paste

600ml (2½ cups) milk

For the orange liqueur cream topping

300ml (1¼ cup) double cream

1 tablespoon orange liqueur

20g (¾oz) flaked almonds, lightly toasted

Working at Harris Tweed Hebrides, islander Margaret Ann knows a thing or two about design and presentation, and this festive showstopper will bring the wow to your table at Christmas. The best part is that you can prepare the jelly, cake and custard on Christmas Eve, so all that's left is to assemble and whip up some cream. If time is of the essence, fear not, as shop-bought Madeira cake and custard will serve as perfect substitutes!

METHOD

To make the marmalade jelly

Dissolve the packet of jelly in a measuring jug with the boiling water, adding the marmalade and stirring until the jelly and marmalade have dissolved. Add the cold water and the orange liqueur, then pour into the trifle bowl. Place in the fridge and after 25 minutes stir the jelly to mix up the marmalade pieces.

About 30 minutes later, place the thin orange slices along the perimeter of the bowl. The aim is to get half the orange slice sitting in the jelly base, so don't add the orange slices until you are confident the jelly mix will support them.

To make the trifle cake

Preheat the oven to 170°C fan (375°F). Grease and line a 20cm x 25cm (8" x 10") rectangular tin.

In a bowl, cream the sugar and butter together, then add the beaten eggs, self-raising flour, baking powder and milk together until you have a smooth and soft batter.

Spoon the mixture into the prepared tin and bake for about 20 minutes until golden and a skewer comes out clean. Turn onto a wire rack and leave to cool completely.

To make the custard

Place the egg yolks, sugar, cornflour and vanilla in a bowl and lightly mix with a fork.

Gently heat the milk in a pan until the mixture is warm. Pour a little of the warm milk into the cold bowl with your egg yolks and use a whisk to beat the milk into the eggs. Add the remainder of the warm milk.

Add the custard mixture to a clean pan and return to a gentle heat. Stir the custard until it thickens to coat the back of a wooden spoon. Set aside to cool with clingfilm over the surface.

To assemble your trifle

For the topping, gently whip the double cream with the orange liqueur until the cream forms soft peaks. Be careful not to over-beat.

Cut the cake into chunks and layer on top of the set jelly. Pour the custard on top to fill in the gaps and then gently scoop the orange cream on top of the custard.

Sprinkle on the toasted flaked almonds and bring to the table. Wow!

YULETIDE SHORTBREAD

MAKES 50

INGREDIENTS

150g (5oz) plain flour

60g (2oz) ground almonds

125g (4½oz) butter, cubed

50g (1¾oz) marzipan, grated

75g (2½oz) sugar

¼ teaspoon almond extract

60g (2oz) flaked almonds

Pinch of fine sea salt

If you share my weakness for marzipan, you'll find these buttery shortbread biscuits to be the perfect accompaniment to a mug of hot chocolate at Christmas. With their melt-in-the-mouth texture and delicate crunch from the flaked almonds, each bite is a blissful combination of festive flavours and textures that will leave you craving more.

METHOD

Preheat the oven to 160°C fan (350°F) and line 2 baking sheets with baking parchment.

Put the flour and ground almonds into a bowl, then rub the butter in with your fingertips until the mixture resembles breadcrumbs. Mix through the grated marzipan, sugar and salt. Add the almond extract and bring the dough together with your hands. Knead for 3 minutes until pliable.

Put the flaked almonds onto a plate.

Take a walnut-sized piece of dough, about 7g (¼oz) in weight, roll it into a ball and press gently into the flaked almonds before placing on the baking sheet and baking for 8 minutes until just golden. Cool on a wire rack and serve with a mug of hot chocolate.

MARMALADE STOLLEN BITES

MAKES 25

INGREDIENTS

100g (3½oz) sultanas

50g (1¾oz) dried cranberries

50g (1¾oz) mixed peel

½ an orange, zested and juiced

100ml (⅓ cup + 2 tablespoons) rum

125ml (½ cup) milk

7g (¼oz) dried active yeast

25g (1oz) sugar

3 cardamom pods, seeded

325g (11½oz) strong white bread flour

½ teaspoon mixed spice

50g (1¾oz) butter, plus extra for brushing

1 egg

1 teaspoon vanilla bean paste

50g (1¾oz) unsalted pistachios, shelled

2 tablespoons marmalade

225g (8oz) marzipan

Pinch of sea salt

Icing sugar, for dusting

Most people's Bucket List might include skydiving, climbing Mount Everest or visiting the Galapagos Islands. Mine? Well, it's a wee bit different. It includes; writing a song for Eurovision and attending the Dresden Stollen Festival. Imagine a day walking around a beautiful city being served hundreds of different styles of stollen? Surely, I can't be the only one? While I wait for that dream to come true, here's how to make this delicious festive treat at home.

METHOD

Place all the dried fruit into a pan with the orange zest. Pour in the orange juice and rum. Over a low heat, allow to simmer gently for a minute, then set aside for an hour.

In a pan, heat the milk until just warm, stir in the yeast and sugar and whisk to combine. Set aside for 5 to 10 minutes, until the yeast has formed a thick, foamy top on the milk.

Grind the cardamom seeds in a pestle and mortar. Add to a bowl along with the flour, mixed spice and a pinch of sea salt. Pour in the milk mix and combine. Then add the butter, egg and vanilla and stir until a sticky dough has formed. Tip onto a floured surface and knead for 10 minutes, or until the dough is smooth and springs back when pressed. Cover the bowl with clingfilm and leave in a warm place for an hour until the dough has doubled in size.

Pour away most of the liquid from the soaked fruit, roughly chop the pistachios and stir in along with the marmalade.

Line a 20cm x 20cm (8" x 8") tin with baking parchment. Sift a teaspoon of icing sugar over a clean surface and roll the marzipan into a 20 cm (8") square.

Tip your dough onto a lightly floured surface, spoon over the fruit and nuts and knead until well combined and the fruits are distributed evenly through the dough. Divide in half. Roll each half out to a rough 20cm (8") square.

Place one half into the tin, top with the marzipan and then lay the second piece of dough on top. Set aside in a warm place to prove for 20 to 30 minutes, until almost doubled in size.

Preheat the oven to 160°C fan (350°F). Bake for 25 to 30 minutes until golden and risen, cool in the tin on a wire rack for 15 minutes, then remove to cool completely. Trim edges and cut into 25 squares. Brush the bites with melted butter before liberally dusting with icing sugar.

MINCEMEAT TRAYBAKE

SERVES 16

INGREDIENTS

For the traybake

180g (6½oz) butter

300g (10½oz) soft brown sugar

1 orange, zested

400g (14oz) mincemeat

1 teaspoon cinnamon

1 egg, beaten

350g (12½oz) self-raising flour

For the buttercream topping

100g (3½oz) white chocolate

200g (7oz) butter

400g (14oz) icing sugar

1 teaspoon vanilla bean paste

To decorate and serve

A handful of white chocolate shavings

A handful of chopped unsalted pistachios

A handful of orange zest

From pies to cookies, ice cream to rocky road, and even festive cocktails, the culinary possibilities of homemade mincemeat are endless. And now, you can add traybakes to that list! It's the perfect way to showcase the delicious flavours of mincemeat, blending its warm spices with a traditional sponge and creamy white chocolate buttercream.

If you're in need of a mincemeat recipe, be sure to check out *The Hebridean Baker: Recipes and Wee Stories from the Scottish Islands* for some inspiration!

METHOD

Preheat the oven to 180°C fan (400°F). Grease and line a 30cm x 20cm (12" x 8") traybake tin.

Melt the butter and sugar in a large saucepan over a low heat, stirring well to ensure that the sugar dissolves. Remove from the heat and allow to cool slightly. Add the orange zest, mincemeat, cinnamon and egg. Stir in the flour and mix thoroughly.

Pour the mixture into the traybake tin and bake for 50 to 55 minutes, or until a skewer inserted into the centre comes out just slightly sticky. Allow to cool in the tin.

To make the buttercream

Break up the chocolate, add half to a bowl and place in the microwave in bursts of 20 seconds until melted, then add the rest of the chocolate and stir until completely melted and allow to cool.

Now place the butter and half the icing sugar in a bowl and beat until smooth. Add the remaining icing sugar and mix until smooth and creamy, then add the vanilla paste and melted white chocolate and mix well.

Remove the traybake from the tin, top with the buttercream, then decorate with white chocolate shavings, chopped pistachios and orange zest.

ARAN NA NOLLAIG

SERVES 8

INGREDIENTS

For the bread

180ml (¾ cup) milk

10g (½oz) dried yeast

450g (1lb) strong white
   bread flour

30g (1oz) sugar

½ teaspoon salt

1 teaspoon ground
   cinnamon

200g (7oz) cream cheese

50g (1¾oz) butter

1 teaspoon vanilla bean
   paste

1 lemon, zested

50g (1¾oz) raisins

50g (1¾oz) glacé cherries

30g (1oz) flaked almonds,
   chopped

1 egg, beaten

For the glaze and
   decoration

100g (3½oz) icing sugar

1 tablespoon lemon juice

2 teaspoons water

30g (1oz) glacé cherries,
   halved

30g (1oz) flaked almonds,
   toasted

Not only does this festive table centrepiece look stunning, but it also tastes absolutely great. This sweet Christmas bread, shaped like a festive wreath, has a delicious golden crust topped with delightful decorations; it's a feast for the eyes and a delight for the taste buds. While I recommend enjoying it on the day it's made, don't fret if there are leftovers. The next day, simply toast it under the grill and spread with lots of butter or jam. Yum!

METHOD

In a pan, heat the milk until just warm, stir in the yeast and whisk to combine. Set aside for 5 minutes.

Add the flour, sugar, salt and cinnamon into a bowl.

Pour the yeasty milk into the flour mixture, then add the cream cheese, butter, vanilla and lemon zest. Using your hands, bring everything together into a rough dough. Tip out onto a floured surface and knead for about 10 minutes.

Place in a bowl, cover with clingfilm and leave in a warm place for an hour until the dough has doubled in size.

Next, tip your dough onto a lightly floured surface, add the raisins, glacé cherries and chopped flaked almonds and knead until well combined and the fruits are distributed evenly through the dough.

Prepare a baking tray by lining it with baking parchment. Take the dough and roll it out on a floured surface, forming it into a long sausage measuring about 30cm (12") in length. Carefully transfer to the baking tray and shape it into a festive wreath, ensuring that the ends are securely joined together.

Cover the wreath with a clean tea towel and let it rise for about 30 minutes. Preheat the oven to 180°C fan (400°F).

Brush the top of the wreath with the beaten egg and bake for about 25 minutes until golden.

Transfer to a wire rack to cool. Once cool, mix the icing sugar, lemon juice and water together. Drizzle the glaze over the top and decorate with your halves of glacé cherries and toasted almonds.

CHRISTMAS MORNING PORRIDGE

SERVES 2

INGREDIENTS

3 cardamom pods

500ml (2 cups) oat or coconut milk, plus a little extra as required

1 chai teabag

1 tablespoon golden syrup

2 whole cloves

1 cinnamon stick

¼ teaspoon ground ginger

120g (4¼oz) rolled oats

35g (1¼oz) sultanas

1 apple

Before the Christmas lunch prep begins and the first bottle of prosecco is opened, it's always good to start the day with a hearty bowl of porridge. Brimming with aromatic spices, this comforting recipe not only sets the perfect tone for the day's festivities but might also become a cherished favourite throughout the year.

METHOD

To make your infusion, crush the cardamom pods lightly and add them to the milk in a pan. Then add the teabag, syrup, cloves, cinnamon stick and ground ginger to the milk. Allow it to simmer on a low heat for 5 minutes, then lift or strain out the whole spices and teabag.

Meanwhile, toast your oats in a dry frying pan over a medium heat for a minute or so.

Add the toasted oats and sultanas to the spiced milk and cook over a medium heat, stirring occasionally, until the oats are tender. If it thickens too quickly, add some more milk.

Grate the apple and stir into the oats, then serve for a wholesome, hearty start to your Christmas morning.

Itheam! Òlam! Caidileam!

LET ME EAT! LET ME DRINK! LET ME SLEEP!

A BAKING PLAYLIST

'S TRUSAIDH MI NA COILLEAGAN
DÀIMH

·

CRAOBH NAN UBHAL
JULIE FOWLIS

·

TEANNAIBH DLÙTH
NITEWORKS (FEATURING SIAN)

·

CAOIDH MHIC SHIRIDH
KIM CARNIE

·

ON THE WINDS OF CHAOS BURN
DUNCAN CHISHOLM

·

LAOIDH NAN BAN
**RACHEL WALKER
& AARON JONES**

·

WRITTEN IN THE SCARS
TIDE LINES

·

PORT NA CAILLICHE
JOY DUNLOP

·

JOURNEYS HOME
RURA

EADAR AN DÀ BHRÀIGH
BREABACH

·

HORO ILLEAN
KATHLEEN MACINNES

·

THE LIGHT OF DAY
TALISK

·

BLÀR INBHIR LÒCHAIDH
**ROBBIE GREIG (FEATURING
EILIDH CORMACK)**

·

THE COMMANDOS' VIEW
GARY INNES

·

ÒRAN A' BHRANNDAIDH
EWEN HENDERSON

·

S I NOCHD A 'CHIAD 'N FHOGHAIR
KAREN MATHESON

·

BEINN A' CHEATHAICH
HÒ RÒ

·

THOIR MO SHORAIDH
THAR GHUNNAIDH'
SKIPINNISH

ACKNOWLEDGEMENTS

Thank you to . . . Ali, Campbell, Thomas and Emma, and all the team at Black & White Publishing and Bonnier Books for allowing me to continue the Hebridean Baker journey!

Seonag, thank you for the bakes, laughs and everything you did to make this book happen; I couldn't have done it without you.

Susie, still the best photographer in the world!

Shona, Mike, Mairi, Iona and all the team at the Isle of Harris Distillery.

Mike, Ruairi and Andy at Jura Whisky, thanks for all the drams, cocktail recipes and wonderful support.

Kirstyn at ERIBÉ Knitwear, Adam & Ruairidh at Loch Duart Salmon. Amy at Highland Stoneware.

Peter and the team at Caledonian MacBrayne for getting me over the Minch and back many times. Shona, Ria and Rona at Charles MacLeod Butchers for keeping me stocked in black puddings!

Margaret Ann at Harris Tweed Hebrides for the festive recipe and the most beautiful tweeds.

Karen Matheson, Douglas Stuart, Janice Forsyth, Eilidh Cormack, Calum MacLean, Anna Campbell-Jones, Joy Dunlop, Lesley Riddoch, Sue Lawrence, Julie Fowlis, Anne McAlpine, Kate MacLeod, Duncan Chisholm, Gary Innes and Katie MacLeod for sharing their Hebridean escapes.

To my brothers Murdo and Colin for sharing their crofting and fishing experience.

Theresa, thank you for baking enough Bonnach Strughain for all of Barra! Angus, the Islay Baker, for all your skills in the kitchen!

Bella Cameron, thanks for the cake and the laughs; DJ and Lindsay Cameron for sharing your love of the croft.

Sandra Watson for a great Canadian/ Scottish/Swiss recipe! Thanks, Ramsey, for sharing your Eriskay cocktail recipe!

Jackie Bruce for your pottery. Brian Ó hEadhra and Goiridh macAlasdair Dhùghaill for your song. Aunt Bellag for sharing your stories. Faye and Robyn for your modelling skills!

Nina, Winnie and everyone at The Park Bar, the best bar in Glasgow!

Sandra and all at Comann Each nan Eilean. Thank you to Ali and Anna from the National Trust for Scotland and the Weaver's Cottage. Thank you to the team at Guardswell Farm.

Taing mhòr do Coinneach Morrison airson a cuid comhairle leis a' Ghàidhlig.

Thanks, Graham, for the accordion playing, Morven and the MacQueens for everything!

And finally, to the most loved pup in Scotland, Seòras.

ABOUT COINNEACH

International bestselling author Coinneach MacLeod was born and raised on the Isle of Lewis, the most northerly of the Outer Hebrides of Scotland. Inspired by traditional family recipes and homegrown produce, the Hebridean Baker cookbooks have made him Scotland's bestselling author of 2021 and 2022. Along the way, he has motivated his worldwide social media followers to bake, forage, learn Gaelic, enjoy a dram or two of whisky and to seek a more wholesome, simple life. Sharing his adventures along with his partner Peter and their Westie pup Seòras, Coinneach's aim is to bring the best of the Scottish islands to a worldwide audience.

You can find Coinneach online at:

hebrideanbaker.com
@hebrideanbaker on Instagram
@hebridean_baker on Twitter
@hebrideanbaker on TikTok

HEBRIDEAN
BAKER